New Directions for
Higher Education

Betsy O. Barefoot
Jillian L. Kinzie
Co-EDITORS

Improving Teaching, Learning, Equity, and Success in Gateway Courses

Andrew K. Koch

EDITOR

Number 180 • Winter 2017
Jossey-Bass
San Francisco

Improving Teaching, Learning, Equity, and Success in Gateway Courses
Andrew K. Koch
New Directions for Higher Education, no. 180
Co-editors: *Betsy O. Barefoot* and *Jillian L. Kinzie*

NEW DIRECTIONS FOR HIGHER EDUCATION, (Print ISSN: 0271-0560; Online ISSN: 1536-0741), is published quarterly by Wiley Subscription Services, Inc., a Wiley Company, 111 River St., Hoboken, NJ 07030-5774 USA.

Postmaster: Send all address changes to NEW DIRECTIONS FOR HIGHER EDUCATION, John Wiley & Sons Inc., C/O The Sheridan Press, PO Box 465, Hanover, PA 17331 USA.

Information for subscribers

New Directions for Higher Education is published in 4 issues per year. Institutional subscription prices for 2017 are:
Print & Online: US$454 (US), US$507 (Canada & Mexico), US$554 (Rest of World), €363 (Europe), £285 (UK). Prices are exclusive of tax. Asia-Pacific GST, Canadian GST/HST and European VAT will be applied at the appropriate rates. For more information on current tax rates, please go to www.wileyonlinelibrary.com/tax-vat. The price includes online access to the current and all online backfiles to January 1st 2013, where available. For other pricing options, including access information and terms and conditions, please visit www.wileyonlinelibrary.com/access.

Delivery Terms and Legal Title

Where the subscription price includes print issues and delivery is to the recipient's address, delivery terms are **Delivered at Place (DAP)**; the recipient is responsible for paying any import duty or taxes. Title to all issues transfers FOB our shipping point, freight prepaid. We will endeavour to fulfil claims for missing or damaged copies within six months of publication, within our reasonable discretion and subject to availability.

Back issues: Single issues from current and recent volumes are available at the current single issue price from cs-journals@wiley.com.

Publisher: New Directions for Student Leadership is published by Wiley Periodicals, Inc., 350 Main St., Malden, MA 02148-5020.

Journal Customer Services: For ordering information, claims and any enquiry concerning your journal subscription please go to www.wileycustomerhelp.com/ask or contact your nearest office.
Americas: Email: cs-journals@wiley.com; Tel: +1 781 388 8598 or +1 800 835 6770 (toll free in the USA & Canada).
Europe, Middle East and Africa: Email: cs-journals@wiley.com; Tel: +44 (0) 1865 778315.
Asia Pacific: Email: cs-journals@wiley.com; Tel: +65 6511 8000.
Japan: For Japanese speaking support, Email: cs-japan@wiley.com.
Visit our Online Customer Help available in 7 languages at www.wileycustomerhelp.com/ask

Production Editor: Abha Mehta (email: abmehta@wiley.com).

Wiley's Corporate Citizenship initiative seeks to address the environmental, social, economic, and ethical challenges faced in our business and which are important to our diverse stakeholder groups. Since launching the initiative, we have focused on sharing our content with those in need, enhancing community philanthropy, reducing our carbon impact, creating global guidelines and best practices for paper use, establishing a vendor code of ethics, and engaging our colleagues and other stakeholders in our efforts. Follow our progress at www.wiley.com/go/citizenship

View this journal online at wileyonlinelibrary.com/journal/he

Wiley is a founding member of the UN-backed HINARI, AGORA, and OARE initiatives. They are now collectively known as Research4Life, making online scientific content available free or at nominal cost to researchers in developing countries. Please visit Wiley's Content Access - Corporate Citizenship site: http://www.wiley.com/WileyCDA/Section/id-390082.html

Printed in the USA by The Sheridan Group.

Address for Editorial Correspondence: Co-editors, Betsy Barefoot and Jillian L. Kinzie, *New Directions for Higher Education*, Email: barefoot@jngi.org

Abstracting and Indexing Services

The Journal is indexed by Academic Search Alumni Edition (EBSCO Publishing); Higher Education Abstracts (Claremont Graduate University); MLA International Bibliography (MLA).

Cover design: Wiley
Cover Images: © Lava 4 images | Shutterstock

For submission instructions, subscription and all other information visit:
wileyonlinelibrary.com/journal/he

CONTENTS

Editor's Notes

Gateway courses—college credit–bearing and/or developmental education courses that enroll large numbers of students and have high rates of Ds, Fs, withdrawals, and incompletes (Koch & Rodier, 2016)—are a ubiquitous part of the undergraduate experience in the United States. As long as there have been U.S. colleges and universities, there have been entry courses that pose difficulties for students—courses that have served more as weeding-out rather than gearing-up experiences for undergraduates. Perhaps the gateway-course weed-out function was more appropriate in the days when a college or university credential was reserved for a privileged few, or even during the era when a high school credential was more than adequate preparation for work and life in a democratic republic. But we no longer live in those times.

I believe that the gateway-course weed-out dynamic is no longer acceptable—if it ever was. Contemporary postsecondary education is characterized by vastly expanded access for historically underserved populations of students, and this new level of access is coupled with increased scrutiny of retention and graduation outcomes. Many of those outcomes are less than desirable. Academic difficulties in gateway courses are particularly pronounced for underserved students who, along with their families, are being expected to bear an increasing portion of the financial burden of postsecondary education. As a result of these less-than-desirable course outcomes and the lower retention rates that correlate with them, policy makers are questioning the investment of public monies in postsecondary education, and students and their families question that value of the college experience itself.

Make no mistake: I am not arguing that a solution to the gateway-course problem is watering down course rigor and content, nor are the other chapter authors in this volume. We believe that those who teach gateway courses and the institutions that offer them must uphold academic standards. But we maintain that they must do so by incorporating the latest evidence-based teaching, learning, and support strategies and by making sure that what happens in the gateway classroom is not contributing to the creation of a permanent underclass. There are tremendous institutional-viability and social-justice implications at play here.

NEW DIRECTIONS FOR HIGHER EDUCATION, no. 180, Winter 2017   © 2017 Wiley Periodicals, Inc.
Published online in Wiley Online Library (wileyonlinelibrary.com) • DOI: 10.1002/he.20256

This volume can serve as a resource for those who seek ways to improve teaching and learning in courses that have historically high failure rates. As a result, the volume can also contribute to the improvement of gateway-course outcomes and completion rates—especially for America's most historically underserved and underprivileged populations that comprise an ever-increasing portion of the student body.

The volume is organized into four parts. In Part I, "The Issue," I define the topic in greater detail in an introductory chapter and make the case for why transforming gateway courses truly matters for the national effort to help more students (especially those who are underserved within higher education) graduate from the colleges and universities where they are admitted (aka the completion agenda).

The second part, "Data-Based Decisions and Actions," includes chapters that share ways that institutional research data and analytics can respectively and collectively be used to improve gateway courses. In Chapter 2, Matthew D. Pistilli and Gregory L. Heileman explore how the promise of analytics—defined as the systematic analysis of data or statistics—can be realized in gateway-course redesign efforts through a combination of good data science and the application of thoughtfully designed, faculty-inclusive processes. The chapter explores matters of institutional readiness for analytics and methods for engaging faculty in applying analytics in course and curriculum redesign.

Chapter 3 details how the institutional research office at North Dakota State University helped the institution identify courses ripe for change, encouraged faculty to employ successful teaching strategies, directed students toward successful learning behaviors, and then assessed the impact of changes made. Authors Emily Berg and Mark Hanson describe how they provided data sources, assessment tools, and research application strategies to advance gateway-course reform. They also offer suggestions on how and why other colleges and universities (and particularly their institutional research offices) should do the same.

Part III, "The Role of Academic Stakeholders," includes chapters that address how academic support, faculty development, academic administration, and discipline associations are vital components of gateway-course improvement efforts. In Chapter 4, Johanna Dvorak and Kathryn Tucker share how and why learning support strategies must be intentionally linked to gateway-course success efforts so that participation in the strategies is not left to chance, putting the most at-risk students in danger. The authors provide successful examples from a regional comprehensive college and an urban research university as well as suggestions for application at other institutions.

Chapter 5 highlights faculty and faculty developers as key actors who can improve student learning and outcomes in gateway courses. Authors Susannah McGowan, Peter Felten, Joshua Caulkins, and Isis Artze-Vega draw on the authors' varied institutional experiences and a large national initiative to outline common challenges, sustainable strategies, and threshold concepts in gateway educational development. They make the case that supporting faculty who teach gateway courses can be a powerful catalyst for transforming an institution's teaching culture.

In Chapter 6, Roberta S. Matthews and Scott Newman make the case that gateway-course transformation efforts should be a top priority for academic leaders because they support and enhance already existing or necessary retention and persistence efforts on campus. The authors provide examples of approaches that senior leaders on campuses of all kinds and sizes may use to engage their campus communities in gateway-course teaching and learning improvement efforts, and offer practical strategies for engaging faculty and staff in the implementation of proven approaches.

Chapter 7 explains why teaching and learning in general or survey courses matter to discipline associations. Authors Julia Brookins and Emily Swafford provide examples of what one such association—the American Historical Association—is doing to promote among its members both contributing to the scholarship of teaching and learning (Boyer, 1990) and its application in the classroom. The chapter also explores why all discipline associations should be concerned and take action to improve undergraduate teaching and learning in their respective discipline's gateway courses.

The last part of this volume, "Integrated Approaches and Systems," includes two chapters that describe how institutions have combined various student success efforts with their gateway-course improvement strategies to increase the likelihood that the strategies are more successful and serve larger numbers of students.

Chapter 8, written by Martine Courant Rife and Christine Conner, provides a case study of how Lansing Community College in Michigan intentionally linked efforts to redesign high-risk courses with the campus's efforts to create Guided Pathways initiatives—specific programs of study supplemented by academic support programs (Bailey, Jaggars, & Jenkins, 2015). The chapter details how the intentional connection between these two initiatives, which are frequently disconnected at many higher education institutions, yielded better results for both efforts and a richer professional and teaching experience for faculty and staff. The chapter also offers considerations for other institutions looking to connect guided-pathways and course-redesign efforts.

In Chapter 9, I, along with my colleagues Richard J. Prystowsky, from Lansing Community College, and Tony Scinta, from Nevada State College, provide examples of how institutions can intentionally link various gateway-course improvement efforts to "make the whole greater than the sum of the parts." Drawing both from lessons learned from the Gardner Institute's Gateways to Completion process and content from the previous chapters of this volume, we make the case that institutions need to purposefully examine all that they are doing, and could be doing, to improve gateway-course outcomes and, where supported by this examination process, rebundle the components into an intentionally interwoven and supportive system to better address the teaching and learning needs of twenty-first-century students.

I thank each of the outstanding chapter authors for their contributions to this volume. Their writing furnishes new and valuable perspectives on the theme of gateway-course improvement. They also meaningfully expand the body of scholarship on this emerging topic and, in the process, provide a rich resource for instructors who teach, staff who support, and administrators who oversee gateway courses and associated continuous quality improvement efforts. It is my sincere hope that you will find as much value in this publication as my colleagues and I derived from writing it.

Andrew K. Koch
Editor

References

Bailey, T. R., Jaggars, S., & Jenkins, P. D. (2015). *What we know about guided pathways.* New York, NY: Columbia University, Community College Research Center. Available from http://ccrc.tc.columbia.edu/media/k2/attachments/What-We-Know-Guided-Pathways.pdf

Boyer, E. L. (1990). *Scholarship reconsidered: Priorities of the professoriate.* Lawrenceville, NJ: Princeton University Press.

Koch, A. K., & Rodier, R. (2016). Gateway courses defined. In A. K. Koch & R. R. Rodier (Eds.), *Gateways to Completion guidebook version 3.0* (p. 6). Brevard, NC: John N. Gardner Institute for Excellence in Undergraduate Education.

ANDREW K. KOCH is the president and chief operating officer of the nonprofit John N. Gardner Institute for Excellence in Undergraduate Education, located in Brevard, North Carolina.

NEW DIRECTIONS FOR HIGHER EDUCATION • DOI: 10.1002/he

PART I. THE ISSUE

This part defines the topic in greater detail in an introductory chapter that makes the case for why transforming gateway courses truly matters for the national effort to help more students succeed, especially those who are underserved within higher education.

1

This introductory chapter defines the phrase gateway courses, *describes why these courses are one of the most compelling issues in the contemporary student success movement, and details what is at stake if the issues associated with these courses are left unaddressed.*

It's About the Gateway Courses: Defining and Contextualizing the Issue

Andrew K. Koch

The Situation

In 1992, political strategist James Carville rallied Bill Clinton's campaign workers around the mantra "It's the economy, stupid." Carville was not attempting to insult anyone's intelligence. Rather, he was making the simple yet profound political point that discussing issues other than the economy would waste resources and time, and probably result in Clinton's defeat. Originally posted on an office wall placard and intended only for the campaign staff, Carville's quip quickly became the de facto slogan for the entire campaign. It helped the Clinton team develop and maintain a focus that ultimately won the election. In years since, "It's the economy, stupid," has become part of American political pundits' vernacular—a mechanism for quickly pinpointing what matters most in an election (Galoozis, 2012).

Carville's mantra and its associated lessons also happen to form the perfect rhetorical concept for explaining why an increased focus on gateway courses—foundational college courses that are high-risk and high-enrollment—is necessary. This volume is intended to provide guidance for the faculty, staff, and administrators in the vanguard of gateway-course improvement who are taking steps to advance and bring to scale this new direction for higher education. I, along with the chapter authors featured in this volume, argue that in 2017, what matters most in the student success movement is our ability to develop and maintain a focus on gateway courses.

Many of us who have worked in and provided thought leadership for the student success movement in the United States over the past 40 years have not paid attention to gateway (or "killer") courses in which students face the greatest risk of poor performance or outright failure. Instead, we

New Directions for Higher Education, no. 180, Winter 2017 © 2017 Wiley Periodicals, Inc.
Published online in Wiley Online Library (wileyonlinelibrary.com) • DOI: 10.1002/he.20257

have focused on other efforts such as learning communities, orientation programs, first-year seminars, and a whole host of other "high-impact practices" (Barefoot et al., 2005; Barefoot, Griffin, & Koch, 2012; Greenfield, Keup, & Gardner, 2013; Koch, 2001; Koch, Foote, Hinkle, Keup, & Pistilli, 2007; Kuh, 2008; Stein Koch, Griffin, & Barefoot, 2013; Upcraft & Gardner, 1989; Upcraft, Gardner, & Barefoot, 2005). To date, these high-impact practices have circumvented the experiences that undergraduates have in gateway courses—experiences that may, in fact, matter most to their success. And until recent years, there has been no concomitant effort to substantively transform the way gateway courses are designed and taught. As a result, failure rates in gateway courses have largely remained unchanged. The effect of these courses can be devastating, particularly for America's least advantaged, first-generation, and historically underrepresented students (Koch, 2017; Koch & Gardner, In Press).

Early student success leaders, however, should not be faulted for their lack of focus on foundational courses. They and their efforts were products of the space, place, and time in which they were operating. David Pace, the accomplished historian and scholar of teaching and learning, aptly described the environment in which student success pioneers were acting. Making his opening comments during a workshop at the 2017 American Historical Association annual meeting, Pace quipped, "In the 1970s and 1980s, the classroom was like the bathroom. You knew something important happened there, and you *never* talked about it!" (Pace, 2017). To date, student success thought leaders have generally focused their actions on activities other than undergraduate courses, including gateway courses, and have had little interaction with faculty.

But this is 2017. And we can now safely say that the sum total of the student success efforts created and initiated in the four-plus decades spanning the late twentieth and early twenty-first centuries have not managed to budge the retention and completion needle in any significant manner. For example, according to ACT, 68.3% of all students who started in a college of any type in fall 1999 returned to that college in fall 2000 (ACT, 2000). In 2015, 15 years later, the rate was 68.0% (ACT, 2015). The good news is that since the 1960s, legislation such as the Civil Rights Act and the Higher Education Acts greatly expanded access to postsecondary education. And contrary to what might have been logically predicted, increased access did not lead to decreases in retention and completion. But neither have there been widespread gains in these outcomes, even though there has been a large influx of state and federal resources to support student success programs.

Thanks to a new and growing body of scholarship on teaching and learning that has emerged over the past decade, we can now point to an array of evidence-based approaches and strategies that have the potential to move student success rates measurably beyond their persistently static level (ACT, 2000, 2015). And unlike most of the efforts that preceded them,

Prescott, B. T. (2008). *Knocking at the college door: Projections of high school graduates by state and race/ethnicity, 1992–2022.* Boulder, CO: Western Interstate Commission for Higher Education.

Prescott, B. T., & Bransberger, P. (2012). *Knocking at the college door: Projections of high school graduates.* Boulder, CO: Western Interstate Commission for Higher Education.

Seymour, E., & Hewitt, N. M. (1997). *Talking about leaving: Why undergraduates leave the sciences.* Boulder, CO: Westview Press.

Stein Koch, S. J., Griffin, B. Q., & Barefoot, B. O. (2013). *National survey of student success initiatives at two-year colleges.* Brevard, NC: John N. Gardner Institute for Excellence in Undergraduate Education. Available from http://www.jngi.org/wordpress/wp-content/uploads/2014/07/National-2-yr-Survey-Booklet_webversion.pdf

University of Missouri Officer of the Registrar. (2017). *Grades, incomplete.* Columbia, MO. Available from http://registrar.missouri.edu/policies-procedures/grades-incomplete-grades.php

Upcraft, M. L., & Gardner, J. N. (1989). *The freshman year experience: Helping students survive and succeed in college.* San Francisco, CA: Jossey-Bass.

Upcraft, M. L., Gardner, J. N., & Barefoot, B. O. (2005). *Challenging and supporting the first-year student: A handbook for improving the first year of college.* San Francisco, CA: Jossey-Bass.

Wells, R. (2008a). Social and cultural capital, race and ethnicity, and college student retention. *Journal of College Student Retention: Research, Theory & Practice, 10*(2), 103–128.

Wells, R. (2008b). The effects of social and cultural capital on student persistence: Are community colleges more meritocratic? *Community College Review, 36*(1), 25–46.

ANDREW K. KOCH *is the president and chief operating officer of the nonprofit John N. Gardner Institute for Excellence in Undergraduate Education, located in Brevard, North Carolina.*

PART II. DATA-BASED DECISIONS AND ACTIONS

This part includes chapters that share how institutional research data and analytics can be respectively and collectively used to improve gateway courses.

2

This chapter provides information on how the promise of analytics can be realized in gateway courses through a combination of good data science and the thoughtful application of outcomes to teaching and learning improvement efforts—especially with and among instructors.

Guiding Early and Often: Using Curricular and Learning Analytics to Shape Teaching, Learning, and Student Success in Gateway Courses

Matthew D. Pistilli, Gregory L. Heileman

The emergence of analytics in higher education institutions is a relatively recent occurrence. While the corporate world has used the nomenclature "business intelligence" for decades, analytics as a term, much less a process, was not used in colleges and universities until Goldstein and Katz (2005) put forth "academic analytics" for the first time (Oster, Lonn, Pistilli, & Brown, 2016). Bischel (2012) defines analytics as "the use of data, statistical analysis, and explanatory and predictive models to gain insights and act on complex issues" (p. 6). Essentially, the goal is to learn things not previously known and to take action on outcomes in an effort to improve.

There are varying levels of analytics (see van Barneveld, Arnold, & Campbell, 2012) described within higher education. Some address the whole institution, some look to predict outcomes, and others look to prescribe select actions that may address various problems and challenges on campus. The specific focus of this chapter is on learning analytics, which focuses on "the measurement, collection, analysis and reporting of data about learners and their contexts, for purposes of understanding and optimizing learning and the environments in which it occurs" (Society of Learning Analytics Research, 2012).

Effective use of learning analytics begins by using relevant data to identify those courses in a curriculum where improvements in learning will yield improved outcomes throughout an entire degree program. That is, it is important to identify early courses in a curriculum that are considered foundational in the major. Improved student success in these gateway courses

NEW DIRECTIONS FOR HIGHER EDUCATION, no. 180, Winter 2017   © 2017 Wiley Periodicals, Inc.
Published online in Wiley Online Library (wileyonlinelibrary.com) • DOI: 10.1002/he.20258

21

provides a vital catalyst toward successful degree completion. Thus, the insights gained through curricular analytics should spur actions that lead to beneficial change at the individual course level. Finally, the loop around the improvement efforts is closed by collecting additional data for assessing the impact of changes and driving additional improvement efforts (Clow, 2012).

Learning analytics holds great promise with regard to creating personalized approaches to learning (Siemens, 2012) or moving education into a space where predictions of student performance can occur (Kellen, 2013), resulting in targeting specific enrichment, tutoring, or supplemental resources to individual students. Lockyer, Heathcote, and Dawson (2013) note that teaching and learning environments are improved through the use of learning analytics, in particular through the redesign of curricula as a result of examining what is and isn't working (Dunbar, Dingle, & Prat-Resina, 2014), and by evaluating the likely impact of possible redesign efforts. Through the improvement of the environment, we are able to demonstrate increases in student performance (Arnold & Pistilli, 2012; Dietz-Uhler & Hurn, 2013; Gray, McGuinness, Owende, & Hofmann, 2016) and student learning (Clow, 2013). As Pistilli, Willis, and Campbell (2014) write, "the institutional application of analytics can result in a major shift for colleges and universities with regard to the culture fostered around undergraduate learning" (p. 88).

This potential for change, however, requires an institution to be ready to move into a realm of data-driven change. Arnold, Lonn, and Pistilli (2014) assert that readiness must be a shared concept understood by individual institutions seeking to create the greatest opportunity for successful implementation. Oster et al. (2016) go further, describing readiness as "a necessary condition for institutions to be able to perform educational functions consistent with their individual missions ... particularly towards student success" (p. 174). The reflective process that Arnold et al. (2014) and Oster et al. (2016) propose is one that any institution should consider using, as it has the potential to produce a great deal of organizational learning involving large swaths of the college or university community.

While there is a need to describe what analytics is and a need for campuses to be ready to implement learning analytics, we also believe that a brief discussion of what analytics *is not* is in order. Analytics in general is not just a fad in higher education; Goldstein and Katz (2005) discussed analytics in 2005, and the marketplace for learning-analytics tools is becoming more and more saturated.

Additionally, analytics is not a solitary process; as Oster et al. (2016) and Pistilli et al. (2014) describe, multiple staff participants from across many different facets of an institution are needed to implement analytics effectively. Finally, as Arnold and Pistilli (2012) note, the development of a learning-analytics solution at any given campus does not have to involve complex algorithms that only statisticians and econometricians understand;

Purdue University's Course Signals (Arnold & Pistilli, 2012), as described later in this chapter, was first developed using Microsoft's Excel and IBM's SPSS products.

Applying Learning Analytics to Gateway Courses

Introductory courses, whether they have a large or a small enrollment, often pose challenges to students. These are usually the courses students new to college encounter in their first terms of study and tend to be the foundation for learning that will occur over the ensuing years. If a student is unable to pass an introductory course in a given discipline, he or she is prevented from taking additional courses within that discipline. Thus, we can think of the introductory courses in a student's major as the most important in terms of their impact on progression toward a degree.

The challenge comes when students—for example, those who have never needed to put a great deal of work into their studies in the past—begin to struggle in these courses. Further, faculty members are often charged with improving outcomes in given courses—that is, ensuring that students are learning and that nonpassing rates are held to a minimum (McCray, DeHaan, & Schuck, 2003). These same faculty members also want to see students succeed in their work; few of them go into the classroom to ensure that students earn Ds or fail. DeBrew and Lewallen (2014) noted that faculty "find that failing a student is stressful" (p. 631) and, as such, would rather avoid having to do so. Faculty obstacles are often related to size and scope—the number of students who should be the focus of an intervention and how a faculty member can intervene effectively and efficiently. In the end, institutions usually seek the same ends as students and faculty: improved learning, improved outcomes, and increased use of resources available to students on campus (Macfadyen & Dawson, 2012). Clearly, there are student-, faculty-, and institution-focused reasons for implementing curricular and learning analytics.

Student-Focused Reasons.   The primary, and often insignificant, change in students who graduate from high school in the spring and start college in the fall is that they are about 3 months older. Typically, during those 3 months, nothing magical happens to make those students self-regulated learners who are acutely aware of how their action or inaction affects the end-of-term outcomes for a given course. Learning analytics may be one way to help new college students develop self-regulation (Siemens, 2012), enhance their understanding of their standing in a course (Fritz, 2013), and, ultimately, improve their own learning and performance (Picciano, 2012). Curricular analytics can be applied to determine the impact these course-level improvements have on overall success rates.

Help-Seeking Behavior.   At its core, help-seeking behavior is rooted in student self-regulation and hinges on students' seeking assistance from appropriate sources when they need it (Corrin, de Barba, & Bakharia, 2017).

NEW DIRECTIONS FOR HIGHER EDUCATION • DOI: 10.1002/he

Baker and Corbett (2014) describe a learning environment in which students are assessed not only on their learning of course material but also on their ability to improve "skills that cut across domains, such as ... help seeking" behavior (p. 39). The use of learning analytics can promote this behavior through interventions such as emails, texts, or phone calls. However, Pardo, Han, and Ellis (2016) caution that if students are not self-regulated enough to take action on feedback, any intervention employed may be unsuccessful; instructors can use learning-analytics-driven interventions (and in-class opportunities) to help students understand the need to visit office hours, attend help sessions, and utilize subject-specific resource rooms on campus (Gray et al., 2016).

Enhancing Students' Understanding of Performance.   Students who understand how their own behaviors relate to their performance have a better chance of being able to alter what they do in an effort to improve their grades. Learning analytics provides an opportunity for giving students feedback about their learning processes. Feedback is defined as an exchange between two or more persons in an effort to better inform individuals' knowledge about their performance, their relative position in a course, and how to enhance their individual work (Tanes, Arnold, Selzer King, & Remnet, 2011). Feedback is beneficial for students as it helps increase students' self-regulation and intellectual curiosity and guides goal setting and achievement (Gray et al., 2016).

Enhancing Faculty's Understanding of Success.   Programs that are designed to ensure that the curricular structure affects student progress have a better chance of being able to provide resources within particular key courses that allow students to overcome obstacles to success. Curricular analytics tools can help program leaders become more aware of the inherent difficulties and bottlenecks within a curriculum and can serve as a guide for applying limited resources most effectively within a curriculum. Furthermore, faculty are more likely to make use of learning analytics within their own courses if they have a big-picture view of how these course-level improvements will influence the overall success of their program.

In order to understand how improvements through learning analytics at the individual level will influence success rates in a course and how this will ultimately influence student success within a program, faculty must have access to aggregate data and statistics. By applying the appropriate analyses to this aggregate data, faculty members can gain a better understanding of when and why particular student populations leave a program, thereby allowing them to focus improvements on the courses most likely to improve overall success outcomes.

Faculty- and Institution-Focused Reasons.   Though the primary reason for implementation of learning analytics by an institution is likely to improve student success, there are other compelling reasons for using learning analytics, especially when it comes to improving outcomes in gateway courses. Those reasons include increasing faculty-to-student communication and improving course outcomes.

Increasing Faculty-to-Student Communication. Chickering and Gamson (1987) describe faculty-to-student communication as one of the best practices associated with undergraduate learning, noting "faculty concern helps students get through rough times and keep on working" (p. 3). Tanes et al. (2011) also found that faculty members who engaged with students using learning analytics saw greater foot traffic during office hours, wherein questions could be answered and guidance provided regarding how to study, what to review, and, if necessary, whether a course should be dropped before the student received a failing grade. It can also be argued that through providing additional information to students, faculty members are able to ensure that students are learning more of what is being taught.

Improving Course Outcomes. It stands to reason that if more students are able to successfully complete a course, then the overall outcomes for the course will increase as well. Macfayden and Dawson (2012) and Arnold and Pistilli (2012) both demonstrate increased course outcomes through the application of learning analytics—in particular, providing feedback to students indicating what they could do to improve their grades. Dietz-Uhler and Hurn (2013) also describe how learning analytics can validate faculty members' intuition about student performance and provide a vehicle for intervening in a timely manner—resulting in improved learning, higher success rates, and increased student persistence toward graduation.

Putting the Action in Actionable Intelligence

Pistilli et al. (2014) assert that learning analytics has the potential to move colleges and universities "from simply understanding various data points and their intersections, to using them to create actionable intelligence" (p. 80). They continue, noting that it is imperative that institutions and faculty take "action on that intelligence as a means of positively affecting one or more behaviors" (p. 80). The most direct action that can be taken is to provide feedback to students, which Astin (1993) notes is something that can improve students' cognitive and personal development, especially if it is fair and encouraging (Lizzio & Wilson, 2008), as well as actionable (Pistilli et al., 2014).

Simply providing feedback is insufficient; feedback must be given both early and often—early enough in the term so that students are able to take action to correct behaviors and improve performance, and often enough for them to see the fruits of their labors (Wise, 2014). Drachsler and Greller (2012) indicate that the potential for increased faculty-to-student interaction is one of the greatest outcomes associated with learning analytics.

When feedback is provided, however, it must be explicit and emphasize outcomes rather than past behaviors (Tanes et al., 2011). It must also be timely; that is, direction needs to be provided to students while they can still employ it (Wise, 2014). At the same time, the tone and rhetoric employed must convey concern for students and be constructive in nature (Lizzio & Wilson, 2008). Feedback also should be brief (Tanes et al., 2011). Failure to observe these conditions may result in students deeming feedback ineffective or ignoring it altogether.

Learning-Analytics Application Examples. Several institutions have had success in developing and implementing learning-analytics solutions that have increased student success and overall outcomes—in particular in, but not limited to, gateway courses and other large enrollment classes.

Check My Activity.   Check My Activity is a tool built into the University of Maryland Baltimore County's learning management system (LMS; Fritz, 2013). When faculty members used the tool, students could see how often they logged into the LMS as compared to their peers, their grades, and the general grades for those who had more or less interaction with the LMS than themselves. Students then used that information to change their approaches to studying, completing work, or seeking assistance, actions that resulted in higher grades.

Course Signals.   Developed at Purdue University and later licensed to Ellucian, Course Signals was one of the first learning-analytics tools deployed at scale. As Arnold and Pistilli (2012) describe, "the premise behind [Course Signals] is fairly simple: Utilize the wealth of data found at an educational institution, including the data collected by instructional tools, to determine in real time which students might be at risk, partially indicated by their effort within a course" (p. 267). The tool provides faculty members a way to reach students in three different categories of risk—high, moderate, and low—and provides guidance and directives to students to help maintain or improve their grades in the course.

Curricular Analytics.   Based on analytical methods developed by researchers at the University of New Mexico (Heileman, Hickman, Slim, & Adballah, 2017), the university created a curricular analytics website (https://curricula.academicdashboards.org). Via this website, users are able to upload the course and prerequisite details associated with a curriculum. The curriculum is then analyzed in order to determine the most crucial courses along with the complexity of the curriculum as a whole. An interactive graphical representation of the entire curriculum is provided, allowing users to investigate individual curricula, evaluate the impact of possible curricular changes, and compare similar curricula at different institutions.

E^2Coach. E^2Coach, developed by researchers at the University of Michigan, provides an "interface between students and the extensive and powerful resources available in each course, customizing recommendations for study habits, assignments for practice, feedback on progress, and encouragement they receive" (McKay, Miller, & Tritz, 2012, p. 90). The tool

delivers personalized feedback to students with information on their work, comparison against their peers' performance, and predictions of final grades should students continue to exert the same effort for the rest of the term.

Student Flow Diagrams.   This tool, developed by researchers at the University of New Mexico (Heileman, Babbitt, & Abdallah, 2015), displays a Sankey diagram that represents the flow of students from a given cohort through a college or university system. The application also allows users to drill down into individual colleges, departments, and programs in order to see how students flow through these units. Through the visual explorations provided by this tool, deductions can be made about success or failure areas of individuals or cohorts of students as they progress through a program. See studentflows.unm.edu for an example.

Implications and Considerations

The contemporary focus on student success is driven by a number of factors that demand our attention, and, at the same time, necessitate careful use of analytics to inform improvement efforts. First, unlike a generation ago, a college degree is now more likely to serve as a precondition to meaningful employment. This has led a significantly larger percentage of high school graduates to now enter college, leading to a much more extensive set of learning needs and student success challenges on college campuses.

Second, as the ability to obtain a college degree has grown in importance, higher education has perversely become much less affordable to most students. The reasons for this are myriad, and well beyond the scope of this chapter, but the net effect is that tuition, books, and room and board costs now routinely add up to more than $25,000 at even lower-cost public colleges, and students are leaving college with unprecedented levels of debt (Heller, 2013; Institute for College Access & Success, 2016).

Thus, we are confronted with the need to serve a broader population of students, with more significant consequences if there is failure at any step in the student journey. In the past, if students failed a class and lost a scholarship, they may have had to work over the summer to earn additional income or take on a few thousand dollars of additional student debt. Today, for many students, a delay in graduation by 1 year can mean $20,000 or more of additional debt, and the loss of a scholarship is a financial catastrophe that often precludes continued enrollment in college.

For these reasons alone, alongside many others not discussed in this chapter, institutions must strive to better meet the needs of their students. This begins by working to gain a more holistic understanding of how the structure of a curriculum affects the specific populations of students attempting to complete that curriculum. From this, we must work to identify those gateway courses that have the largest impact on student success and then apply learning analytics to empower the success of the students in these courses. In this way, through a judicious use of data science applied to curricula and a thoughtful application of these outcomes to teaching and learning improvements, the promise of analytics in higher education is realized.

References

Arnold, K. E., Lonn, S., & Pistilli, M. D. (2014, March). An exercise in institutional reflection: The Learning Analytics Readiness Instrument (LARI). In A. Pardo & S. Teasley (Eds.), *Proceedings from the 4th International Conference on Learning Analytics and Knowledge* (pp. 163–167). New York, NY: ACM. https://doi.org/10.1145/2567574.2567621

Arnold, K. E., & Pistilli, M. D. (2012, April). Course Signals at Purdue: Using learning analytics to increase student success. In D. Gašević, S. Buckingham Shum, & R. Ferguson (Eds.), *Proceedings from the 2nd International Learning Analytics & Knowledge Conference* (pp. 267–270). New York, NY: ACM. https://doi.org/10.1145/2330601.2330666

Astin, A. W. (1993). What matters in college? *Liberal Education, 79*(4), 4–16.

Baker, R. S., & Corbett, A. T. (2014). Assessment of robust learning in educational data mining. *Research & Practice in Assessment, 9,* 38–50.

Bischel, J. (2012). *Analytics in higher education: Barriers, progress, and recommendations* [Research report]. Littleton, CO: EDUCAUSE Center for Applied Research. Available from http://net.educause.edu/ir/library/pdf/ERS1207/ers1207.pdf

Chickering, A. W., & Gamson, Z. F. (1987). Seven principles for good practice in undergraduate education. *AAHE Bulletin, 39*(7), 3–7.

Clow, D. (2012, April). The learning analytics cycle: Closing the loop effectively. In D. Gašević, S. Buckingham Shum, & R. Ferguson (Eds.), *Proceedings from the 2nd International Learning Analytics & Knowledge Conference* (pp. 134–138). New York, NY: ACM. https://doi.org/10.1145/2330601.2330636

Clow, D. (2013). An overview of learning analytics. *Teaching in Higher Education, 18*(6), 683–695. https://doi.org/10.1080/13562517.2013.827653

Corrin, L., de Barba, P. G., & Bakharia, A. (2017, March). Using learning analytics to explore help-seeking learning profiles in MOOCs. In X. Ochoa, I. Molenaar, & S. Dawson (Eds.), *Proceedings of the 7th International Learning Analytics & Knowledge Conference* (pp. 424–428), New York, NY: ACM. https://doi.org/10.1145/3027385.3027448

DeBrew, J. K., & Lewallen, L. P. (2014). To pass or to fail? Understanding the process used by nurse educators in the clinical setting. *Nurse Education Today, 34*(4), 631–636. https://doi.org/10.1016/j.nedt.2013.05.014

Dietz-Uhler, B., & Hurn, J. E. (2013). Using learning analytics to predict (and improve) student success: A faculty perspective. *Journal of Interactive Online Learning, 12*(1), 17–26.

Drachsler, H., & Greller, W. (2012, April). The pulse of learning analytics: Understandings and expectations from the stakeholders. In D. Gašević, S. Buckingham Shum, & R. Ferguson (Eds.), *Proceedings from the 2nd International Learning Analytics & Knowledge Conference,* pp. 120–129. New York, NY: ACM. https://doi.org/10.1145/2330601.2330634

Dunbar, R. L., Dingel, M. J., & Prat-Resina, X. (2014). Connecting analytics and curriculum design: Process and outcomes of building a tool to browse data relevant to course designers. *Journal of Learning Analytics, 1*(3), 223–234.

Fritz, J. (2013, April). *Using analytics at UMBC: Encouraging student responsibility and identifying effective course designs* [Research bulletin]. Littleton, CO: EDUCAUSE Center for Applied Research. Available from https://library.educause.edu/~/media/files/library/2013/4/erb1304-pdf.pdf

Goldstein, P. J., & Katz, R. N. (2005). *Academic analytics: The uses of management information and technology in higher education.* Littleton, CO: EDUCAUSE Center for Applied Research. Available from https://library.educause.edu/~/media/files/library/2005/12/ers0508w-pdf.pdf

Gray, G., McGuinness, C., Owende, P., & Hofmann, M. (2016). Learning factor models of students at risk of failing in the early stage of tertiary education. *Journal of Learning Analytics, 3*(2), 330–372. https://doi.org/10.18608/jla.2016.32.20

Heileman, G. L., Babbitt, T., & Abdallah, C. T. (2015). Visualizing student flows: Busting myths about student movement and success. *Change: The Magazine of Higher Learning 47*(3), 30–39.

Heileman, G. L., Hickman, M., Slim, A., & Abdallah, C. T. (2017, June). Characterizing the complexity of curricular patterns in engineering programs. *Proceedings of the 2017 American Society for Engineering Education (ASEE) Annual Conference,* Columbus, Ohio.

Heller, D. E. (Ed.). (2013). *The states and public higher education policy: Affordability, access, and accountability* (2nd ed.). Baltimore, MD: Johns Hopkins University Press.

Institute for College Access & Success. (2016). *Student debt and the class of 2015: 11th annual report.* Oakland, CA: Author. Available from http://ticas.org/sites/default/files/pub_files/classof2015.pdf

Kellen, D. A. (2013). *Utilizing technology as leverage for instructional improvement in the classroom* (Unpublished doctoral dissertation). University of Michigan, Ann Arbor. Available from https://deepblue.lib.umich.edu/bitstream/handle/2027.42/97866/dkellen_1.pdf

Lizzio, A., & Wilson, K. (2008). Feedback on assessment: Students' perceptions of quality and effectiveness. *Assessment & Evaluation in Higher Education, 33*(3), 263–275.

Lockyer, L., Heathcote, E., & Dawson, S. (2013). Informing pedagogical action: Aligning learning analytics with learning design. *American Behavioral Scientist, 57*(10), 1439–1459. https://doi.org/10.1177/0002764213479367

Macfadyen, L. P., & Dawson, S. (2012). Numbers are not enough: Why e-learning analytics failed to inform an institutional strategic plan. *Educational Technology & Society, 15*(3), 149–163.

McCray, R. A., DeHaan, R. L., & Schuck, J. A. (Eds.). (2003). *Improving undergraduate instruction in science, technology, engineering, and mathematics: Report of a workshop.* Washington, DC: National Academies Press.

McKay, T., Miller, K., & Tritz, J. (2012, April). What to do with actionable intelligence: E²Coach as an intervention. In D. Gašević, S. Buckingham Shum, & R. Ferguson (Eds.), *Proceedings from the 2nd International Learning Analytics & Knowledge Conference* (pp. 88–91). New York, NY: ACM. https://doi.org/10.1145/2330601.2330627

Oster, M., Lonn, S., Pistilli, M. D., & Brown, M. G. (2016, July). The Learning Analytics Readiness Instrument. In S. Dawson, H. Drachsler, & C. P. Rosé (Eds.), *Proceedings from the 6th International Conference on Learning Analytics and Knowledge* (pp. 173–182), New York, NY: ACM. https://doi.org/10.1145/2883851.2883925

Pardo, A., Han, F., & Ellis, R. A. (2016, July). Exploring the relation between self-regulation, online activities, and academic performance: A case study. In S. Dawson, H. Drachsler, & C. P. Rosé (Eds.), *Proceedings from the 6th International Conference on Learning Analytics and Knowledge* (pp. 422–429), New York, NY: ACM. https://doi.org/10.1145/2883851.2883883

Picciano, A. G. (2012). The evolution of big data and learning analytics in American higher education. *Journal of Asynchronous Learning Networks, 16*(3), 9–20.

Pistilli, M. D., Willis, J. E., III, & Campbell, J. P. (2014). Analytics through an institutional lens: Definition, theory, design, and impact. In J. A. Larusson & B. White (Eds.), *Learning analytics: From research to practice* (pp. 79–101). New York, NY: Springer Science+Business Media. https://doi.org/10.1007/978-1-4614-3305-7_5

Siemens, G. (2012, April). Learning analytics: Envisioning a research discipline and a domain of practice. In D. Gašević, S. Buckingham Shum, & R. Ferguson (Eds.), *Proceedings from the 2nd International Learning Analytics & Knowledge Conference* (pp. 4–8). New York, NY: ACM. https://doi.org/10.1145/2330601.2330605

Society of Learning Analytics Research. (2012). About [Webpage]. Available from http://www.solaresearch.org/mission/about/

Tanes, Z., Arnold, K., Selzer King, A., & Remnet, M. A. (2011). Using Signals for appropriate feedback: Perceptions and practices. *Computers & Education, 57,* 2414–2422. https://doi.org/10.1016/j.compedu.2011.05.016

van Barneveld, A., Arnold, K. E., & Campbell, J. P. (2012). *Analytics in higher education: Establishing a common language* (ELI Paper 1: 2012). Littleton, CO: EDUCAUSE. Available from http://net.educause.edu/ir/library/pdf/ELI3026.pdf

Wise, A. F. (2014, March). Designing pedagogical interventions to support student use of learning analytics. In S. Teasley & A. Pardo (Eds.), *Proceedings of the 4th International Conference on Learning Analytics and Knowledge* (pp. 203–211), New York, NY: ACM. https://doi.org/10.1145/2567574.2567588

Matthew D. Pistilli is the director of student affairs assessment and research in the division of student affairs at Iowa State University.

Gregory L. Heileman is professor of electrical and computer engineering and associate provost for student and academic life at the University of Kentucky.

3

This chapter provides an example of how one university's institutional research office played an active role in using data from institutional studies to guide the university toward courses ripe for change, faculty toward successful teaching strategies, students toward successful learning behaviors, and the university toward assessing the impact of the changes.

Putting the "Evidence" in Evidence-Based: Utilizing Institutional Research to Drive Gateway-Course Reform

Emily A. Berg, Mark Hanson

A New Vision for Institutional Research

Today's higher education landscape necessitates that organizational change be driven by evidence-based decision making. Offices of institutional research (IR) have historically helped facilitate decision making by being resources for data collection, study, and dissemination (Saupe, 1990) as well as organizational intelligence (Fincher, 1978). Thorpe (1999) identified "internal reporting" and "planning support" to be the most frequent phrases used in a study of the content of 63 IR offices' mission statements. In recent years, transparency and accountability requirements have reinforced the importance of IR offices with regard to compliance reporting. A more important, but often secondary, role for IR offices is that of change agent and organizational learning facilitator.

Transformative organizational change is slow and complex, and it happens most effectively when members involved in and affected by the change see value in change implementation (Poole & Van de Ven, 2004). Different perspectives about a single issue can lead to different interpretations and understandings of facts (Birnbaum, 1988). Colleges and universities are dynamic organizations that have a multitude of perspectives about the nature of challenges and how they should be resolved. Collaboration between campus actors is critical for organizational learning to fully consider these varied perspectives; however, the siloed nature of institutions is a key obstacle to institutional improvement. IR offices have the opportunity and

NEW DIRECTIONS FOR HIGHER EDUCATION, no. 180, Winter 2017   © 2017 Wiley Periodicals, Inc.
Published online in Wiley Online Library (wileyonlinelibrary.com) • DOI: 10.1002/he.20259

responsibility to reach across the institution to bring those with varied perspectives together to focus on important issues (Voorhees & Hinds, 2012).

IR has recently shifted from a mostly passive model of reporting toward a proactive model of engagement (Volkwein, 2008). The cross-campus work of IR builds natural systems of collaboration, horizontal connections, and organizational learning that can be shared broadly to improve collaboration among campus constituents (Leimer, 2009). In this model, IR offices are active members of the campus community and are called on not just for their familiarity with and access to campus data, but for their insights, high-level institutional knowledge, and ability to connect seemingly disparate institutional data and research. Illustrating this updated vision of IR, the Association for Institutional Research (AIR) recently released a comprehensive statement of aspirational practices. Swing and Ross (2016) challenge IR professionals to have a broader view of who is a decision maker and to work directly with students, staff, and faculty rather than maintain a traditional exclusive focus on campus administrators alone. They also refocus the IR mission as one that is grounded in a student-focused paradigm. From this philosophical vantage point, IR has a natural and important role to play in student success efforts in general and in gateway-course reform initiatives in particular.

The Role of IR in Gateway-Course Reform

Important decision points relating to courses occur on a daily basis for all campus actors. Students, faculty, administrators, and staff are involved in a complex series of actions and relationships that ultimately culminate in the success, or nonsuccess, of a student in a course. Each stakeholder's actions are important in determining outcomes; therefore, IR can be of most use by targeting support at every level involved. Decision points range from pointed and short-term (e.g., a student's academic behavior decisions) to broad and ongoing (e.g., an administrator's decisions about which courses need support and how to support them). The cumulative effect of this support from IR may lead to small changes by each actor and substantial measurable change on a collective scale.

We contend that IR can and should play a key role in bringing attention to areas where change is needed, informing what changes are called for, and assessing the impact of changes made. IR offices are well suited to help lead their campuses in efforts to improve student course outcomes in a comprehensive, cross-disciplinary, and cross-campus manner. In a practical sense, IR offices are often able to function nicely as neutral resources because they are often situated under an institution's chief academic officer rather than in any one academic unit (Swing, Jones, & Ross, 2016) and have experience and expertise in research design, survey construction, administration, interpretation, and reporting.

NEW DIRECTIONS FOR HIGHER EDUCATION • DOI: 10.1002/he

Institutional Context

North Dakota State University (NDSU) began an ongoing era of conscientious monitoring of nonpassing/unsatisfactory grade rates (D, F, or W) in gateway courses in 2010. At this time, a revision of general education curricula brought to light a number of courses, many of which were critical to student success, that yielded higher-than-desirable nonpassing grade rates. Institutional surveys and studies have consistently identified areas for improvement suggesting that support for student success in gateway courses may translate to improved student success overall. However, at this institution, responsibility for implementing and/or monitoring these changes was not recognized as belonging to one person or group. As a result, actions to facilitate improvements were not undertaken in a way that recognized the institutional level of concern. Additionally, decentralized oversight of general academic student success created institutional challenges with regard to broad organizational monitoring and improvement, as well as understanding and addressing institutional norms.

At NDSU, the IR office reports to the provost, and studies undertaken by IR are focused mainly on academic affairs. The office approaches data and analyses as informational and nonbiased; in other words, data are allowed to tell the story, rather than having the data located to support a preformulated story. The studies reported here coincided with NDSU's participation as one of 13 pilot institutions in the John N. Gardner Institute's Gateways to Completion program, a 3-year structured course-reform effort.

Supporting the Life Cycle of Gateway-Course Reform

While more studies than can be detailed in this chapter led to significant improvements in course outcomes in four gateway courses, the following framework explains a series of studies that empowered decision makers to use institutional evidence to bring about fruitful change. The framework includes using evidence to (a) identify courses in need of change, (b) determine how to change them, (c) encourage positive student academic behaviors, and (d) assess the impact of changes made.

Evidence Guiding Us Toward Which Courses to Improve

We used various methods to prioritize courses on which reform efforts should be focused. Particular attention was paid to a combination of historical enrollment totals and rates of D, F, and W (DFW) grades. The largest potential for negative impact is in courses with both high enrollment and high rates of DFW grades. While it is true, for example, that 2,130 DFW grades were earned over a 5-year period in College Composition (the course with the highest undergraduate enrollment on campus), the course's overall DFW grade rate was just 17%. If a reasonable grade distribution is maintained, there is not significant room for improvement. Introductory Psychology, in contrast, awarded 3,284 DFW grades over the same 5-year period and had a DFW rate above 30%. A drop of 10% in the proportion of students earning DFW grades in this course would result in a substantially larger number of students completing a general education requirement and progressing in their education.

To make this clear for administrators and instructional faculty, a simple histogram was prepared showing the top 30 undergraduate courses on campus awarding the highest number of DFW grades over a 5-year period. Each course was assigned one of three colors indicating whether its DFW grade rate was greater than 30% (red), between 20% and 29% (yellow), or less than 20% (green). The height of the bar for each course represented the number of DFW grades earned by students over a 5-year period and ranged from 687 DFW grades in a computer science course to 3,617 DFW grades in college algebra. The histogram allowed course outcomes to be easily compared and evaluated—highlighting areas for the largest potential impact.

A more sophisticated approach helped us further target course-reform work. A research analyst skilled at using a combination of cell formulas, pivot tables, and Microsoft Visual Basic for Application (VBA) created a dynamic Excel dashboard presentation of courses on campus with high enrollment and high DFW grade rates. By clicking a few straightforward filters, instructors were able to instantly assess how student enrollment and grade outcomes varied by course delivery method (face-to-face or online), fall or spring semester, course instructor, student class level (first-year through senior), student major, and whether students were repeating the course for a second, third, or fourth time. Using the dashboard, a group of instructional faculty and staff working to reform an introductory history course were quickly able (in less than 30 minutes) to gain these four insights:

1. Students taking the course online had a 13% higher DFW rate than students taking it face-to-face.
2. First-year students made up nearly two thirds of the course enrollment and had the highest rate of DFW grades.
3. Students repeating the course had high DFW grade rates of 63% and 71% on their second and third tries, respectively.
4. Only 2% of students taking the course over a 5-year period were history majors.

The small number of history majors enrolled in the course was perhaps the most surprising insight and led to reconceptualizing the course as a general education credit rather than an introduction to history for history majors.

Based on this and other early successes with a dashboard format, our IR office now uses the data analysis system Tableau to make a wide variety of dashboards available to the campus. One dashboard, in particular, reports student grade distributions segmented by a variety of demographics (e.g., gender, race, citizenship status, first-generation status, and Pell eligibility). Instructional faculty currently working on course reform have found these data helpful as they consider the differential impact that pedagogy may have on students from a variety of backgrounds.

Evidence Guiding Us Toward Effective Pedagogy

With some understanding of the courses in which students struggled the most, there was interest in a better understanding of why students were struggling. Individuals in different roles on campus offered different anecdotal explanations, and all likely explain a portion of reality: Students come to college underprepared, admission standards should be higher, course enrollments are too large, students seem disengaged, and so on. Rather than relying on assumptions alone, a course-reform group worked with the IR office to gather survey data directly from 591 students in two gateway courses—Introductory Chemistry and Introductory History.

Along with quantitative Likert-scale satisfaction items, much of the survey asked open-ended questions eliciting rich qualitative feedback from students. Students' responses explained factors, from their point of view, that influenced their grade, their quality of preparation for the course, course content they found difficult, and their ideas about how to improve the course overall. Through a qualitative data-analysis process of coding statements, identifying themes and subthemes, and quantifying the occurrence of each, students' responses identified several on-target action items.

A primary insight was that students held themselves accountable for their grades. There were nearly twice as many comments about the impact of their own effort ($n = 398$) than the next most commonly reported theme, which consisted of their opinions and perceptions of the quality of their professor ($n = 209$). Students said their grades were largely a result of time spent studying, attending class, completing homework, and utilizing out-of-class support resources. This corroborates other NDSU IR research showing that students are not satisfied with lower grades and are interested in their academic performance (Office of Institutional Research and Analysis, 2017). This information was counterintuitive to those assuming that underperformers simply do not care about their academic performance and, in part, helped our group's conversation move toward more constructive explanations for why students struggle in gateway courses.

Students also articulately confirmed what we know to be true about shortcomings related to the passive large lecture and the many advantages associated with active-learning pedagogies (see Froyd, 2007). Both of the courses in question have sections of 200 to 400 students and have historically relied on a traditional PowerPoint lecture paired with four or five exams over the course of the semester. Central themes in the feedback suggested students' desire for more interaction with their peers and the instructor, time in class to actually practice and work through examples together, chances to relate the material to real-life issues, and more opportunities to demonstrate their learning, and feeling unsure of how to be successful in the course. A student wrote, "Change up the way the course is taught ... there needs to be more interaction and explanation in class, instead of just reading off the slides." Very few comments (2% of all comments) noted disinterest in the subject matter as a primary determinant of the final grade.

This feedback pairs nicely with active-learning research, including that of Aitken (2005), who noted:

> While lecturing may continue to be an important component to teaching, these studies recommend that courses be redesigned to include at least the following pedagogical components: (a) active-learning experiences, (b) frequent assessment of learning, (c) meaningful and frequent feedback to students on their learning process, and (d) relating course content to the personal experience of students. (p. 61)

Packaging the survey results with representative literature made a compelling case to instructors and department chairs reluctant to invest in change and helped us identify initial targets for how things needed to change.

Evidence Guiding Students Toward Effective Behaviors

Kuh, Cruce, Shoup, Kinzie, and Gonyea (2008) found that students can improve their likelihood of succeeding in college by engaging in positive academic behaviors, such as preparing for and attending class, completing course assignments, and spending sufficient time learning the material on their own outside of class. Faculty and staff participants in NDSU's gateway-course reform program during fall 2014 were interested in understanding academic behaviors of successful students within specific courses. The National Survey of Student Engagement (NSSE) measures student engagement through survey questions about academic and nonacademic behaviors and experiences. Validity and reliability studies of NSSE suggest that it is a high-quality instrument for measuring student behaviors associated with academic success (see http://www.nsse.indiana.edu/html/psychometric_portfolio.cfm). NDSU participated in NSSE eight times between 2000 and 2013, yielding a large volume of data readily available for analysis. Consistency of NDSU's NSSE results has contributed to the NDSU community's high level of confidence in the use of NSSE data as reliable evidence of student behavioral practices at this institution.

For this study, we selected 11 items from the 2011 and 2013 NSSE surveys that reflected course-related behavioral practices that could be independently modified by the student. For example, "Hours spent studying outside of class" was included because students can directly affect their own behavior through more or less studying. Other items, such as "Number of short papers written," were excluded because an outside factor (instructor requirements) may heavily influence the students' answers.

The study population included students enrolled in the four lower-level, high-enrollment courses of interest in fall 2012 and fall 2013 semesters. Items on the NSSE instrument ask the students to consider their experiences over the past year, and those experiences were compared to final course grades (including recorded course withdrawals) that were collected from the institutional student information system. "Successful" students were defined as those who earned grades of A or B in a course; "Unsuccessful" students were those earning a grade of D or F. Grades of C and W were excluded from this study. To determine reported behavioral differences between students who were successful versus those who were unsuccessful in a course, NSSE item means were calculated for students who earned A or B grades (successful) and for students who earned D or F grades (unsuccessful) for each of the four courses.

Students who were successful in a course generally engaged in positive academic behaviors at higher rates than their unsuccessful peers, although differences between groups varied by course, suggesting that students who succeed in a course are able to discern which academic behaviors were most important for success within that particular course. For example, successful students in Human Anatomy more often asked another student to help them understand course material, whereas students successful in Introductory Chemistry did not. The results of this study were shared with course faculty and program leadership. One faculty member used survey results to develop a "Top Ten Ways to Succeed in This Course" document, which was shared with students at the beginning of the following term. As with the aforementioned studies, this innovative work guided the conversation toward focusing on student behaviors. Instructors held discussions about their need to play a proactive role in helping students understand, in a specific way, how to be successful in a particular course rather than assuming that all students knew the level of effort required to be successful. Continued conversations about student academic behavior led to new or strengthened relationships between instructors and academic resources, such as the campus tutoring center and writing center.

Evidence to Assess Our Progress

Course-reform progress was assessed by tracking student grade distributions over time. The Student Assessment of Learning Gains (SALG) survey (Seymour, Wiese, Hunter, & Daffinrud, 2000) was also used to collect a significant amount of longitudinal within-course data directly from students in order to ascertain how their experiences in class shifted as a result of the pedagogical changes being made. Because of low response rates to on-line surveys, feedback was gathered from students in person in each section of each class engaged in the course-reform effort. This amounted to more than 3,000 completed SALG surveys from students in four gateway courses between fall 2013 and fall 2015.

The SALG survey (Seymour et al., 2000), employed by the Gardner In-stitute in the Gateways to Completion process, asks students to reflect on their learning over the course of the semester and to consider how certain aspects of the course affected their learning. The survey included questions on topic integration, class discussion, group work, class activities, assess-ment feedback, and guidance from the instructor on how to be successful in the course. A small group of IR staff administered the survey in paper and pencil format during the final 3 weeks of each semester. The course instructor was asked to leave the room for 10 minutes, and the anonymous assessment was framed as a part of work our IR office routinely does to gather information from students to assess how things are going on cam-pus.

Over 98% of students completed the survey, and results were instruc-tive. On the whole, students were more satisfied with several aspects of each of the courses involved; in some cases, changes were dramatic. Results were segmented by course section and instructor and compiled into sim-ple bar chart visuals showing changes on each item over the 3-year period. One question, for example, asks students how helpful discussions during class are to their learning. Each successive class of students in Introduc-tory Psychology viewed classroom discussion more favorably over three fall semesters. Item means and statistical tests of significance for changes from one year to the next were significant and informative to the instruc-tor because they confirmed that his efforts to incrementally introduce small group discussion into lecture sections of more than 350 students had been effective.

Grade outcomes were also tracked over time. Instructors and adminis-trators were initially provided rates of DFW grades as a baseline and then updated rates for each year of the course-reform effort. It is difficult for in-structors to account for withdrawals over time because the students disap-pear from their electronic grade books when they withdraw from a course. IR offices have access to grades in all courses, so it is quite efficient to com-pile and chart grade rates over time. The four courses involved improved from a combined baseline DFW rate of 36% to 24% after 3 years of course-reform work.

Conclusions and Recommendations

Having an active role in this reform effort improved course outcomes by informing the work with local evidence at each point in the process. IR had a seat at the table rather than passively filling data requests for someone in a work group without having an in-depth understanding of the context and goals for the request. This improved the quality, quantity, and depth of research questions asked and answered. Given that IR staff are generally in tune with campus data and research resources, they are able to help groups formulate questions and research strategies they would not otherwise consider. Putting data directly in the hands of those wanting to take action at all levels of the organization dramatically increases the likelihood of follow-up action.

IR's involvement in this work has also had a ripple effect on other areas of campus. IR's choices to actively investigate and report some areas in more depth than others helped, and continues to help, shape consensus about our campus student success agenda. Focus and investment in teaching and learning on campus has increased as evidenced by the development of an Office of Teaching and Learning and the implementation of a National Science Foundation grant to improve instruction by providing pedagogical training for more than 150 faculty over a 5-year period. Institutional data were leveraged in each case to build consensus and make the case that change was both necessary and possible. Student learning and outcomes have remained a key focus of our work on campus.

For institutions wishing to make better use of IR offices in the process of evidence-based gateway-course reform, we respectfully offer the following recommendations:

- *For institutional leaders:* Work to involve institutional researchers at all levels of the change process, and consistently advocate for using evidence in the campus decision-making processes.
- *For faculty and staff:* The IR office has access to a lot of information about students on campus that can be shaped to better understand how they perform in a number of contexts and the factors that drive their outcomes. This information can be a powerful guide to selecting approaches to teaching and student support.
- *For IR offices:* Be proactive with outreach and get to know main actors on campus. Make an effort to know the context of issues and campus goals, and report data in a way that is easily accessible to those on campus who can use it to create change, no matter the scale. Have personal conversations with people about the data rather than assuming they will learn what they need to know from a report.

IR staff members have the skill, knowledge, opportunity, and now the responsibility to use the data at their fingertips to create and share both simple and sophisticated analyses that can have a positive impact on student success in gateway courses.

New Directions for Higher Education • DOI: 10.1002/he

References

Aitken, N. (2005). The large lecture course redesign project: Pedagogical goals and assessment results. *College Teaching Methods & Styles Journal, 1*(2), 61–68.

Birnbaum, R. (1988). *How colleges work.* San Francisco, CA: Jossey-Bass.

Fincher, C. (1978). Institutional research as organizational intelligence. *Research in Higher Education, 8*(2), 189–192.

Froyd, J. (2007). *Evidence for the efficacy of student-active learning pedagogies.* Retrieved from http://cte.virginia.edu/wp-content/uploads/2013/07/Evidence-for-Efficacy-Froyd.pdf

Kuh, G. D., Cruce, T. M., Shoup, R., Kinzie, J., & Gonyea, R. M. (2008). Unmasking the effects of student engagement on first-year college grades and persistence. *Journal of Higher Education, 79*(5), 540–563.

Leimer, C. (2009). Taking a broader view: Using institutional research's natural qualities for transformation. In C. Leimer (Ed.), *New Directions for Institutional Research: No. 143. Imagining the future of institutional research* (pp. 85–93). San Francisco, CA: Jossey-Bass.

Office of Institutional Research and Analysis. (2017, January 10). *STEPS to success: An academic social norming campaign.* Retrieved from https://www.ndsu.edu/fileadmin/oira/STEPS_Campus_Report.pdf

Poole, M., & Van de Ven, A. (2004). *Handbook of organizational change and innovation.* New York, NY: Oxford University Press.

Saupe, J. L. (1990). *The functions of institutional research* (2nd ed.). Tallahassee, FL: Association for Institutional Research.

Seymour, E., Wiese, D., Hunter, A., & Daffinrud, S. (2000, March). *Creating a better mousetrap: On-line student assessment of their learning gains.* Paper presented at the National Meeting of the American Chemical Society, San Francisco, CA.

Swing, R. L., Jones, D., & Ross, L. E. (2016). *The AIR national survey of institutional research offices.* Tallahassee, FL: Association for Institutional Research. Retrieved from http://www.airweb.org/nationalsurvey

Swing, R. L., & Ross, L. E. (2016). *Statement of aspirational practice for institutional research.* Tallahassee, FL: Association for Institutional Research. Retrieved from http://www.airweb.org/aspirationalstatement

Thorpe, S. W. (1999, November). *The mission of institutional research.* Paper presented at the Conference of the North East Association for Institutional Research, Newport, RI.

Volkwein, J. F. (2008). The foundations and evolution of institutional research. In D. Terkla (Ed.), *New Directions for Higher Education: No. 141. Institutional research: More than just data* (pp. 5–20). San Francisco, CA: Jossey-Bass.

Voorhees, R. A., & Hinds, T. (2012). Out of the box and out of the office: Institutional research for changing times. In R. D. Howard, G. W. McLaughlin, & W. E. Knight (Eds.), *The handbook of institutional research* (pp. 73–85). San Francisco, CA: Jossey-Bass.

EMILY A. BERG *is the director of institutional research and analysis at North Dakota State University.*

MARK HANSON *is the associate director of institutional research and analysis at North Dakota State University.*

PART III. THE ROLE OF ACADEMIC STAKEHOLDERS

This part includes chapters that respectively address how academic support, faculty development, academic administration, and discipline associations are vital components of gateway-course improvement efforts.

4

This chapter describes how peer learning support programs can be used to improve learning and success in gateway courses. It provides examples from two institutions to further illustrate how this promising approach can improve student outcomes.

The Case for Intentionally Interwoven Peer Learning Supports in Gateway-Course Improvement Efforts

Johanna Dvorak, Kathryn Tucker

Tutoring has been a mainstay of college academic support for much of the history of U.S. higher education (Arendale, 2010). While tutoring began as a service for the elite, it took on a remedial connotation as a result of mass education. Beginning in the 1970s and 1980s, however, learning centers and writing centers began to reject the remedial label (Arendale, 2010; Harris, 1988/2006; North, 1984), and today there is high interest in normalizing the use of academic support as successful student behavior (Louis, 2015). To that end, more intentional academic-support services are being offered on college campuses. The programs may be designed by a learning center or developed as a collaboration of stakeholders. Advisors, instructors, and faculty can encourage, incentivize, or require participation in cooperation with the support service.

What Is Intentionally Interwoven Peer Learning Support?

As we define it, intentionally interwoven peer learning support formally involves peers (other students) in the delivery of support. Peer support has a special role in gateway courses, since peer support leaders are usually embedded in the courses. But peer support may also connect to other settings that involve the faculty, curriculum, and pedagogy. These range from collaborations between faculty and writing or tutoring centers on a single course project to sustained linking to a course via workshops or class visits, to embedded tutoring, and to unique connections that fit local needs. Certainly, the ways these links evolve vary widely. The two most widely used models are supplemental instruction and writing fellows.

New Directions for Higher Education, no. 180, Winter 2017 © 2017 Wiley Periodicals, Inc.
Published online in Wiley Online Library (wileyonlinelibrary.com) • DOI: 10.1002/he.20260

Supplemental Instruction. Supplemental instruction (SI), which began in 1973 at the University of Missouri–Kansas City (UMKC), is the most established of these intentional approaches (University of Missouri–Kansas City, 2017). The focus on specific "historically difficult courses" differentiates SI from tutoring models. Rather than targeting high-risk students, SI supervisors target high-risk courses. Most of these are high-enrollment large lecture courses, many of which are gateway courses to a major. These courses generally enroll significant numbers of first- and second-year students. The peer SI leader, who has previously taken the course and has usually earned an A, attends the lectures and leads three to four weekly group reviews to discuss course content and incorporate college-study strategies. SI leaders work closely with faculty, read class assignments, take notes in class, and serve as role models (Arendale, 1994; University of Missouri–Kansas City, 2017).

Because SI participants generally outperform their peers, those who oversee variations of the SI model and other embedded learning-assistance initiatives are working to increase attendance in the initiatives themselves. The National Science Foundation has supported one model, peer-led team learning (PLTL). In this model, groups of eight students, led by peer leaders, are required to meet an additional hour beyond the lecture to solve assigned problems as a group (City College of New York, Center for Peer-Led Team Learning, 2017). Peer-assisted learning (PAL) at the University of Minnesota follows the SI model closely but has modified it to incorporate PLTL and other learning-assistance models (Arendale, 2014, University of Minnesota, 2017). In Structured Learning Assistance (SLA) (Ferris State University, n.d.), students are required to attend additional peer-led group review sessions. Finally, tutoring services have also become more intentional in including in-class tutoring for "flipped" or active learning classrooms. In the Emporium model, for example, lab tutors are assigned to assist students individually as they work on individualized computer math programs (National Center for Academic Transformation, n.d.).

Writing Fellows. Rather than building knowledge of material that will be demonstrated on an exam, students in writing-instructive or writing-intensive courses build skills to express themselves effectively on topics and for audiences relevant to the course. Practically speaking, this difference means that peer tutors may work with students on the same assignment for weeks and need different strategies from those used in SI.

Writing fellows programs trace their history to Brown University and Carleton College in the late 1970s and early 1980s; in these programs, the directors articulated efforts to provide embedded peer support for writing across the curriculum (Haring-Smith, 1992/2000). Programs inspired by Brown's or Carleton's models may be referred to as writing fellows, curriculum-based peer tutoring, or embedded writing tutoring. Writing fellows are writing tutors who are attached to or embedded in a specific course and provide feedback on student drafts to emphasize the process of conversation, drafting, feedback, and revision. While writing fellows may be students who have previously succeeded in the course, many programs embed trained writing tutors who have not taken the course they will support, and the original concept at Brown intentionally placed fellows in courses they had *not* taken to avoid having fellows confused with graders or teaching assistants (Haring-Smith, 1992/2000). Support for writing may be attached to writing-instructive courses, such as first-year composition classes, where learning to write is a significant course objective. Support for writing may instead, or also, be attached to writing-intensive courses, where writing to learn is a significant aspect of course instruction (Colorado State University, WAC Clearinghouse, 2017).

One aspect these programs have in common is training. Since Boylan, Bliss, and Bonham (1997) found that "tutoring with training" was the variable that made the difference for students' academic success, training has become an integral part of learning-support programs.

Two Cases of Integrated Interventions

University of Wisconsin–Milwaukee. The University of Wisconsin–Milwaukee (UWM), an urban research university of 26,000 students, is located just north of downtown Milwaukee along Lake Michigan. Most of its 4,000 first-year students live in UWM residence halls while 6,000 students live in the surrounding neighborhood. Only 60 years old, the campus is part of the University of Wisconsin system and is designated as a Research I Institution. Because of its access mission, serving underprepared students is a strong focus. The campus is the most diverse in the state, with multicultural students constituting 33% of its enrollment. Thirty-nine percent of undergraduates are first-generation students. Over 95% of the incoming first-year students are traditional age, but many of them already are juggling school, work, and parenting (University of Wisconsin–Milwaukee, 2016).

UWM's Panther Academic Support Services (PASS) has taken a proactive approach to supporting college students in their first 2 years. Its SI program expanded from four SI sections in 1995 to 50 SI sections each semester in 2004 when the University of Wisconsin–Milwaukee's Access to Success (A2S) initiative began funding the SI program. Seventy-five PASS tutors also hold weekly group tutoring sessions. Walk-in and online tutoring is also available, as well as a virtual learning center with study strategies and course-related online resources in four PASS virtual learning management system (LMS) course sites (University of Wisconsin–Milwaukee, 2017).

SI leaders at UWM are juniors, seniors, or graduate students who have excelled in the course, earned at least a 3.0 grade point average (GPA), and have a professor's recommendation and excellent communication skills. Most SI leaders have earned a 3.5 GPA and an A in the course, often with the same professor. The UMKC certified PASS staff trains its SI leaders and tutors together; tutors often become SI leaders as they gain experience (University of Wisconsin–Milwaukee, 2017). PASS SI leaders and tutors are certified through the College Reading and Learning Association's (CRLA) International Tutor Training Certification Program (College Reading and Learning Association, 2017). SI leaders complete additional training following the UMKC SI Supervisor/Leader Training model (University of Wisconsin–Milwaukee, 2017). The PASS SI program is also certified by the National Association for Developmental Education (NADE) for course-based learning assistance programs (National Association for Developmental Education, 2017).

While face-to-face academic support is still the most popular service, PASS has intentionally increased access for UWM students to online learning support. PASS has been a leader in providing online academic-support services using its own tutors and SI leaders since 2002. Students enrolled in on-campus gateway courses are making strong use of the PASS online or blended sessions for SI. Using the synchronous web-conferencing platform, Blackboard Collaborate, participants can communicate virtually using two-way video, audio, or chat tools, draw on whiteboards, browse the Internet, or share documents. SI leaders conduct weekly blended sessions or online exam reviews. Students can review session archives in one of the PASS online course sites (Dvorak, 2017).

On-campus marketing has been successful in making PASS a welcome environment for all students. The PASS website and LMS course sites, direct emails, and social media market directly to students. While services are not mandatory, faculty members support PASS by recommending SI leaders, meeting regularly with SI leaders, and promoting SI to their students. Some give extra credit for SI participation.

Nevada State College.   Nevada State College (NSC) is a teaching college founded in 2002 to create a middle tier in Nevada's public higher education system between the 2-year colleges and the two research universities, University of Nevada Reno and University of Nevada Las Vegas. NSC is located in Henderson, about a 25-minute drive from downtown Las Vegas. The campus has grown steadily, enrolling 3,700 commuter and online students in fall 2016. NSC's access mission is reflected in the student body: 62% are the first generation in their family to attend college, 75% are women, 53% identify as ethnic minority, 55% are nontraditional age with 17% of incoming first-year students aged 25 and up, and 76% are eligible to participate in the Federal TRIO Student Support Services program (Nevada State College, 2017). Students navigate work, family, health concerns, poverty, and the challenges of valuing their long-term goals over their immediate needs.

The course assistant program at NSC began as an outgrowth of the college's participation in the John N. Gardner Institute's Gateways to Completion (G2C) project. The program weaves together peer mentoring, peer tutoring, and SI strategies, using undergraduate peers to support student academic learning while addressing other risk factors associated with high rates of Ds, Fs, and withdrawals. Like SI leaders, course assistants (CAs) are attached to a course and, despite the similarity of their title to teaching assistants, are there to support but not teach students. CAs attend the course, offer office hours and individual appointments, design and provide at least two collaborative learning workshops per week, meet with faculty, meet with a program mentor, participate in weekly ongoing professional development, and do outreach to students in their courses, usually working a minimum of 15 hours per week. The program training encourages CAs to look for opportunities to connect with their students, so their work happens during both formal interactions and informal conversations.

Course assistants have at least 1 year's experience at NSC, have maintained at least a 3.0 GPA during the previous year, and have earned a B+ or better in the course in which they will assist.

They participate in 20 hours of presemester training and complete an additional 8 or more hours of program-specific training. During the semester, they meet weekly for ongoing training. Training topics include mind-set (Dweck, 2006), understanding and addressing risk factors in the experiences of first-generation and nontraditional students, data-supported successful study strategies, bridging to campus resources, and building self-efficacy.

Students' interaction with their CAs is entirely voluntary outside of class. Most faculty teaching CA-enhanced courses include the CA in activities during class, ranging from asking the CA to model a problem or provide support during lab to dedicating class time for a CA-designed and faculty-approved collaborative workshop. CAs report better attendance at their workshops outside class when faculty include them during class, making close collaboration between CAs and faculty essential. Because course assistants collaborate so closely with faculty, it was determined the program needed leadership from current teaching faculty, and the course assistant program director must maintain a record of excellence in the classroom.

Successes and Challenges

The research on the success of college learning-assistance efforts has been hindered by the variation and duplication of academic support initiatives, numerous names of services, and lack of consistent research methods. Nonetheless, efforts have been made to compile extensive bibliographies of research on peer learning programs (Arendale, 2016; Learning Support Centers in Higher Education [LSCHE], 2017) and writing fellows programs (Lauckner, Hughes, Hall, Reglin, & Zawacki, 2011). SI has withstood the test of time since 1973; regular student participants earn one half grade to one full grade higher and have better retention rates than nonparticipants (University of Missouri–Kansas City, 2017). While a review of research of SI programs from 2001 to 2010 (Dawson, Van der Meer, Skalicky, & Cowley,

2014) found these claims justified, researchers recommended (1) more controls in studying SI outcomes to account for variations in SI programs and research methods and (2) compulsory SI to improve student participation.

Writing fellows programs similarly show positive outcomes. Song and Richter (1997) found that students with in-class tutors experienced significantly higher pass rates and higher apparent rates of persistence and skill transfer than those without in-class tutoring. Qualitative results on writing fellows programs include stronger connections between faculty and student services (Masiello & Hayward, 1991); increased use of student services (Severino & Knight, 2007); more positive attitudes about writing from students and faculty (Haring-Smith, 1992/2000; Kinkead, 1993); higher rates of faculty satisfaction with student writing (Haring-Smith, 1992/2000; Kinkead, 1993); and broader institutional change (Condon & Rutz, 2012; Corroy, 2003).

Results for SI participants at UWM mirror national data of higher participant-course grades. SI has been one of the most successful retention interventions at UVM, with 80% to 90% persistence rates for first-year SI cohorts over the past 12 years. Only honors and undergraduate research programs, which selected top students, maintained the same retention rates. Due to SI's consistent effectiveness, UWM is intentional about using SI as a support strategy for student learning and success strategies. A collaboration between PASS, faculty, and the UWM faculty Center for Excellence in Teaching and Learning (CETL) is making an effort to reduce the DFW rates for gateway courses by 20% (Reddy, 2016). Faculty members are taking a larger stake in the process to increase student success by making SI a more integral part of gateway courses.

The first 3 years of the course assistant program at Nevada State College have shown significant promise, primarily in the areas of retention, connection with other academic services, and influence on campus culture. All data were retrieved from the Nevada State College Profile (Nevada State College, 2017). One-year retention rates are over 8% higher for students who have taken a CA-enhanced course than for the general student population. Students in CA-enhanced courses also pass at higher rates and engage in successful student behaviors, such as using other academic services at a rate that is 16% higher than those who have not had a CA-enhanced course. NSC students who use academic services average a GPA over 3.0, compared with an average GPA below 2.5 for students who do not use services. Finally, the CA program has drawn attention campus-wide, inspiring a similar program in the School of Nursing and collaborations with the School of Education, and generating faculty and student requests for more CA-enhanced courses, as well as for other types of peer support. The presemester training to prepare CAs now includes peer support staff from more than 10 programs and departments, encouraging collaboration and collegiality across campus. Students have noticed the impact of CA-enhanced courses as well. In end-of-semester surveys, students in CA-enhanced courses convey their increased sense of belonging and self-efficacy, noting that the college's clear commitment to their success helped them feel confident they could, in fact, succeed.

Peer academic support benefits peer leaders as well. Peer tutors solidify their own knowledge and develop their leadership skills (Dvorak, 2001). Arendale's bibliography (2017) delineates effects of peer cooperative-learning groups on facilitators in the areas of increased confidence, academic achievement, personal and professional development, and leadership development. These include a wide array of peer-led academic-support interventions as well as more intentional models of peer-leader development. For example, Arendale and Hanes (2016) describe how peer-assisted learning (PAL) leaders at the University of Minnesota developed their leadership and group facilitation skills from their training and experience. The Peer Writing Tutor Alumni Research Project provides a survey and methods for anyone seeking to learn more about how their own tutors have learned from their work (Hughes, Gillespie, & Kail, 2017). Sample results such as those from the University of Wisconsin–Madison offer rich description and reflective narratives ("From UW-Madison Writing Fellows Alumni") showcasing critical thinking skills and reporting the alumni's abilities to draw on their time as tutors in their personal and professional lives (University of Wisconsin–Madison, 2017).

The positive outcomes for program participants have led to calls for mandatory attendance in learning-support programs. While mandatory attendance would make research easier and has shown many of the same positive outcomes as voluntary attendance (Mas, 2014), several complications should be considered. For some campuses, mandatory attendance for learning supports is cost prohibitive. While funding for integrated support usually comes from student-success fees or tuition, it may, however, be possible to secure external donations or grants for initial phases of new programs. These programs are more likely to be supported internally once local data demonstrate program effects. Mandatory attendance may also pose challenges for students. Adding required time on campus, particularly at institutions with a large commuter population or high numbers of nontraditional students, can cause intense stress. Transparent scheduling during course registration and making mandatory sessions available online allow students more agency and flexibility; online models, however, require additional technology and training.

Staffing itself can be a challenge, with or without mandatory attendance. Staff members face low pay rates, student turnover, high GPA requirements, short hiring time frames, schedule conflicts, and lack of space. Although online-learning supports may resolve the space issue, these require specialized training. Supervisors themselves may need additional training to provide effective support for staff who are, first and foremost, students. Staff members must also encourage faculty collaboration, communication, and trust between faculty members and their peer leaders. Roles and responsibilities must be clearly defined, and reporting structures should be reasonable and transparent.

Conclusion

Intentionally interwoven learning supports show great promise in increasing student engagement, persistence, and graduation. They may be considered high-impact interventions, improving outcomes not only for students in targeted courses but also for peer leaders providing services, faculty teaching the courses, and the broader campus culture. While interwoven services can be resource-intense, their impact beyond the single course can justify their cost. In designing intentional support, institutions should consider local variables, such as student population, budget, space, and training needs to select or adapt the versions that will best fit their needs. Intentional learning-support interventions can help to erase the deficit model of academic support and engage many more students in a successful college academic experience. This cannot be accomplished by learning-center and writing-center professionals alone. Faculty and higher-level administration backing is crucial to promoting and funding these services. With students, their peer leaders, academic support personnel, faculty, and administration working together, an investment in intentional academic support is capable of increasing college student success and creating future leaders.

References

Arendale, D. R. (1994). Understanding the supplemental instruction (SI) model. In D. C. Martin & D. R. Arendale (Eds.), *New Directions for Teaching and Learning: No. 60. Supplemental instruction: Increasing student achievement and retention* (pp. 11–21). San Francisco, CA: Jossey-Bass. Retrieved from http://doi.org/10.1992/tl.e7219946004

Arendale, D. R. (2010). *Access at the crossroads: Learning assistance in higher education.* San Francisco, CA: Jossey-Bass.

Arendale, D. R. (2014). Understanding the peer assisted learning model: Student study groups in challenging college courses. *International Journal of Higher Education, 3*(2), 1–12. Retrieved from http://www.sciedu/journal/index.php/ijhe/article/view/4151/2498

Arendale, D. R. (2016). Postsecondary peer cooperative learning groups: Annotated bibliography. Retrieved from http://www.arendale.org/peer-learning-bib/

Arendale, D. R., & Hanes, A. (2016). Adaptation and flexibility when conducting and planning peer study group review sessions. *Learning Assistance Review, 21*(2), 9–37.

Boylan, H. R., Bliss, L., & Bonham, B. (1997). Program components and their relationship to student performance. *Journal of Developmental Education, 20*(3), 2–9.

City College of New York, Center for Peer-Led Team Learning. (2017). *Peer-led team learning.* Retrieved on June 10, 2017, from https://sites.google.com/site/quickpltl/

College Reading and Learning Association (CRLA). (2017). *International tutor training program certification.* Retrieved from http://crla.net/index.php/certifications/ittpc -international-tutor-training-program

Colorado State University, WAC Clearinghouse. (2017). *Writing fellows programs.* Retrieved from https://wac.colostate.edu/fellows/

Condon, W., & Rutz, C. (2012). A taxonomy of writing across the curriculum programs: Evolving to serve broader agendas. *College Composition and Communication*, 64(2), 357–382. Retrieved from http://www.ncte.org/library/nctefiles/resources/journals/ccc/0642-dec2012/ccc0642taxonomy.pdf

Corroy, J. (2003). Institutional change and the University of Wisconsin–Madison Writing Fellows Program. *Young Scholars in Writing*, 1, 25–44. Retrieved from http://arc.lib.montana.edu/ojs/index.php/Young-Scholars-In-Writing/article/view /75/37

Dawson, P., Van der Meer, J., Skalicky, J., & Cowley, K. (2014). On the effectiveness of supplemental instruction: A systematic review of supplemental instruction and peer-assisted study sessions literature between 2001 and 2010. *Review of Educational Research*, 84(4), 609–639.

Dvorak, J. (2001). The college tutoring experience. *Learning Assistance Review*, 6(2), 33–46.

Dvorak, J. (2017). *Successful practices for developing online tutoring services: A CRLA webinar*. Retrieved on June 10, 2010, from http://www.crla.net/

Dweck, C. S. (2006). *Mindset*. New York, NY: Random House.

Ferris State University. (n.d.). *Structured learning assistance*. Retrieved from http://www.ferris.edu/sla/

Haring-Smith, T. (1992/2000). Changing students' attitudes: Writing fellows programs. In S. H. McLeod & M. Soven (Eds.), *Writing across the curriculum: A guide to developing programs* (pp. 123–131). Newbury Park, CA: SAGE. Retrieved from https://wac.colostate.edu/books/mcleod_soven/chapter11.pdf

Harris, M. (2006). *The concept of a writing center*. International Writing Centers Association. Retrieved from http://writingcenters.org/writing-center-concept-by-muriel-harris/ (Original work published 1988 by the National Council of Teachers of English)

Hughes, B., Gillespie, P., & Kail, H. (2017). *The peer writing tutor alumni research project*. Retrieved June 10, 2017, from https://writing.wisc.edu/pwtarp/

Kinkead, J. A. (1993). Taking tutoring on the road: Utah State University's Rhetoric Associates Program. In J. A. Kinkead & J. G. Harris (Eds.), *Writing centers in context: Twelve case studies* (pp. 210–215). Retrieved from http://files.eric.ed.gov/fulltext/ED361707.pdf

Lauckner, J., Hughes, B., Hall, E., Reglin, J., & Zawacki, T. (2011). *Writing fellows programs bibliography*. Fort Collins, CO: WAC Clearinghouse. Retrieved from https://wac.colostate.edu/fellows/bib.cfm

Learning Support Centers in Higher Education (LSCHE). (2017). *LSCHE*. Retrieved from http://wwwlsche.net

Louis, M. C. (2015). Enhancing intellectual development and academic success in college: Insights and strategies from positive psychology. In J. C. Wade, L. I. Marks, & R. D. Hetzel (Eds.), *Positive psychology on the college campus* (pp. 99–131). Retrieved from http://www.reader.eblib.com.ozone.nsc.edu

Mas, C. V. (2014). Supplemental instruction as a mandatory lab component for developmental education courses at community colleges. *Supplemental Instruction Journal*, 1(1), 22–37.

Masiello, L., & Hayward, M. (1991). The faculty survey: Identifying bridges between the classroom and the writing center. *Writing Center Journal*, 11(2), 73–79. Retrieved from http://casebuilder.rhet.ualr.edu/wcrp/publications/wcj/wcj11.2/wcj11.2_Masiello_Hayward.pdf

National Association for Developmental Education. (2017). *National Association for Developmental Education course-based learning assistance*. Retrieved from https://nadeaccredation.net/resources/applicant-resources

NEW DIRECTIONS FOR HIGHER EDUCATION • DOI: 10.1002/he

National Center for Academic Transformation. (n.d.). *How to redesign a developmental math program by using the Emporium Model.* Retrieved from http://www.thencat.org/Guides/DevMath/DM1.%20The%20Essential%20Elements%20of%20the%20Emporium%20Model.pdf

Nevada State College. (2017). *Nevada State College profile.* Retrieved from https://public.tableau.com/profile/nevadastatecollege#!/vizhome/Dashboard4_0_0/NSC

North, S. (1984). The idea of a writing center. *College English, 46*(5), 433–446. Retrieved from http://www.jstor.org/stable/377047

Reddy, D. M. (2016). *Summary of student learning & success strategies.* Unpublished report, University of Wisconsin–Milwaukee.

Severino, C., & Knight, M. (2007). Exporting writing center pedagogy: Writing fellows programs as ambassadors for the writing center. In W. J. Macauley & N. Mauriello (Eds.), *Marginal words, marginal work* (pp. 19–34). New York, NY: Hampton.

Song, B., & Richter, E. (1997). Tutoring in the classroom: A quantitative study. *Writing Center Journal, 18*(1), 50–60. Retrieved from http://www.jstor.org/stable/43442036

University of Minnesota. (2017). *Peer-assisted learning (PAL).* Retrieved from: https://www.lib.umn.edu/smart/peer-assisted-learning-pal

University of Missouri–Kansas City. (2017). *Supplemental instruction.* Retrieved from http://www.info.umkc.edu/si/

University of Wisconsin–Madison. (2017, March 6). *Another word—from the writing center at the University of Wisconsin–Madison.* Retrieved from https://writing.wisc.edu/blog/?cat=36

University of Wisconsin–Milwaukee. (2016). *Semester enrollment, fall 2016.* Retrieved from http://www.uwm.edu/institutional-research/semesterenrollment/

University of Wisconsin–Milwaukee. (2017). *Panther Academic Support Services (PASS).* Retrieved from http://uwm.edu/pass

JOHANNA DVORAK is the emerita director of Panther Academic Support Services at the University of Wisconsin–Milwaukee.

KATHRYN TUCKER is assistant professor of English and director of the writing center at Nevada State College.

NEW DIRECTIONS FOR HIGHER EDUCATION • DOI: 10.1002/he

Faculty and faculty developers can improve student learning and outcomes in gateway courses by improving course design, integrating active learning, and aligning assessments with course goals. Drawing on the authors' varied experiences and a large national initiative, this chapter outlines challenges and strategies to support gateway-course faculty development.

5

Fostering Evidence-Informed Teaching in Crucial Classes: Faculty Development in Gateway Courses

Susannah McGowan, Peter Felten, Joshua Caulkins, Isis Artze-Vega

Freeman et al. (2014) wrote an influential meta-analysis of research on active learning in higher education science, technology, engineering, and math (STEM) classrooms. In their conclusion, they implore faculty to integrate active learning into their teaching: "If the experiments analyzed here had been conducted as randomized controlled trials of medical interventions, they may have been stopped for *benefit*" (p. 8413). Students learn more in, and are more likely to successfully complete, STEM courses that incorporate active-learning pedagogies. Building on these findings, we contend that evidence-informed course design is an ethical imperative in all gateway courses. Powerful research demonstrates the efficacy of specific strategies; why aren't we all implementing these pedagogies in our gateway courses? This chapter explores this question through specific cases to illustrate how faculty development can play a critical role in providing support and generating cultural change toward evidence-informed teaching and active learning in gateway courses.

Why Focus Faculty Development on Gateway Courses?

As has been established in the earlier chapters of this volume, gateway courses are characterized by high enrollment and high withdrawal/failure rates (Eagan & Jaeger, 2008; Koch, 2017). They represent roadblocks to student persistence and timely graduation, and differentially affect students from underrepresented groups, discouraging them from continuing

NEW DIRECTIONS FOR HIGHER EDUCATION, no. 180, Winter 2017 © 2017 Wiley Periodicals, Inc.
Published online in Wiley Online Library (wileyonlinelibrary.com) • DOI: 10.1002/he.20261

in higher education (Perna & Jones, 2013). While many complex factors contribute to gateway-course outcomes, faculty are an essential element of any gateway-course reform. Faculty typically determine the pedagogies and assessment methods in these classes, and they also act as agents in first-year student socialization and academic engagement (Evenbeck & Jackson, 2005).

To imbue gateway-course instructors with so much responsibility yields additional issues in terms of staffing. Gateway courses often are taught by part-time or non-tenure-track faculty and graduate student instructors (Bailey, Jaggers, & Jenkins, 2015), which can contribute to pedagogical and evaluative inconsistency between sections. Additionally, the frequent turnover in the instructors who teach gateway courses threatens the sustainability of enhancement initiatives around course design, active learning, and assessment.

Gateway-course faculty development offers an opportunity to improve student learning by working across three levels: individual, departmental, and institutional. Evenbeck and Jackson (2005) emphasize that gateway-course redesign "is often the ideal context for transforming faculty culture" because so many faculty members teach or have an interest in the student outcomes developed in these foundational courses (after all, faculty who teach upper-level courses will be working with the students who enrolled in gateway courses in previous terms). A recent study at Washington State University and Carleton College underscored the significance of this kind of capacity-building related to teaching and learning: "A generative culture multiplies the impact of formal faculty development, enhances self-motivated, individual faculty learning, and supports faculty experimentation in their courses" (Condon, Iverson, Manduca, Rutz, & Willett, 2016, p. 121). Empowering faculty at the grassroots of this cultural change is the foundation of the faculty-development efforts we describe in the following cases.

Three Cases of Gateway-Course Faculty Development

In this section, we present three case studies of faculty-development efforts focused on gateway courses. The first explores a single gateway course at the University of Rhode Island. The second outlines an institution-wide initiative on gateway-course reform at Florida International University. The third considers a national project that involves hundreds of faculty at scores of institutions, the Teaching and Learning Academy offered by the John N. Gardner Institute for Excellence in Undergraduate Education (JNGI). In these three cases, we will highlight some of the distinct contextual factors and common themes that shape gateway-course faculty development.

University of Rhode Island.   The University of Rhode Island (URI) is the largest public institution in the state; in 2016, 14,801 undergraduates and 3,303 graduate students enrolled. URI recognizes, like other institutions of similar size, that many students struggle to earn productive grades in gateway courses, especially in STEM disciplines.

In 2013, URI participated as a founding institution in JNGI's Gateways to Completion (G2C) program. G2C involves a close examination of five gateway courses with a pattern of high nonproductive grade rates (i.e., D, F, W [withdrawal], and I [incomplete] grades). A steering committee directs the campus-wide initiative to support the work of each course-level committee, consisting of faculty and staff closest to and most directly involved with each gateway course.

For example, Kimberly Fournier, an assistant professor within the department of kinesiology, coordinated BIO 121, a human anatomy class with 500 to 600 students each semester that is known generally as a "weeder" course. Many health-related programs at URI require a grade of C or better in this course for students to advance in the curriculum. Professor Fournier recognized that students often feel acute anxiety associated with course content and exam difficulty, so she sought ways to improve student study skills while maintaining academic rigor. She used the G2C program as an opportunity to redesign the course; she hoped her efforts would improve learning for all of her students, and she particularly hoped to increase the number of students who would learn enough to earn grades that would propel them into their chosen fields of study.

Fournier chaired the BIO 121 course-level committee composed of faculty from many disciplines who taught the course or taught courses that required BIO 121 as a prerequisite. The committee included a faculty developer (Joshua Caulkins, coauthor of this chapter) and a staff member from the URI Academic Enhancement Center. Over the course of one semester, the committee agreed upon key recommendations that included ensuring consistency across sections, improving alignment with later courses, and establishing a closer partnership with the unit that offers supplemental and tutoring instruction.

Over the next 2 years, Fournier and Caulkins pursued two specific evidence-based strategies to improve study skills in order to reduce student anxiety. First, they introduced two-stage testing (e.g., collaborative testing) to the course, specifically designed to reorient assessment as part of the learning process and to reduce test anxiety in students (Pandey & Kapitanoff, 2011; Stearns, 1996). Second, they integrated in-class active learning activities into lectures. Despite the large class size, Professor Fournier and her colleagues used scaffolded worksheets in class to guide students through applied exercises that built on prior knowledge. This work gave students deliberate practice in the knowledge and problem-solving skills they needed in the course and in future courses.

As detailed in a recently published article (Fournier, Couret, Ramsay, & Caulkins (2017), some students experienced reduced test anxiety, although this result was not universal. Nonproductive grade rates were reduced from 23% during the 2012–2013 academic year to 13% during the intervention, and to 15% in the subsequent two semesters. Fournier viewed the G2C program as a way to make positive changes to her course that she and her colleagues are committed to continuing.

Florida International University.   Classified as a both a Highest Research Activity Doctoral University and a Hispanic-serving institution (HSI), Florida International University (FIU) enrolled 41,000 students in the fall of 2016. Of these, 67% identified as Hispanic/Latino and 12% as African American/Black. The decision to concentrate on gateway courses reflected the needs of the university's distinctive student population. Most FIU students live at home, not on campus, and have many competing demands for their time, including familial responsibilities and work. The university determined that its retention initiatives must meet students where they are: in classrooms. From 2012 to 2015, gateway-course enrollment accounted for approximately 18,600 course enrollments per year for first-year cohorts of about 4,300 students.

Early initiatives in FIU's gateway-course redesign efforts focused on college algebra, a course that had a failure rate of 70% for the decade prior to 2011. Through a program supported by the U.S. Department of Education, instructors shifted to student-centered instruction, resulting in a passing rate increase to 20% by fall 2012.

Determined to ease students' transition to academia and improve their retention, FIU joined URI in 2013 in the G2C program. Initially, the university focused on five courses, but in 2014, it expanded course redesign efforts to 17 high-enrollment (>1,600), high-failure (>15%), and/or high-impact (strong predictor of dropping out or delayed graduation) courses.

With support from the Association of Public and Land Grant Universities and the Coalition of Urban Serving Universities, the FIU Center for the Advancement of Teaching (CAT) created varied mechanisms for advancing gateway-course redesign: CAT created incentivized opportunities for faculty in all 17 gateway courses—100 faculty in 2013 alone. CAT hosted luncheons to bring together department chairs and FIU's office of institutional research to design a gateway-course survey that has been used to capture the experiences of more than 9,000 students to date, providing institutional-, course-, and instructor-level data to inform continued improvement.

Since fall 2012, the percentage of first-time-in-college students who pass all of the gateway courses they take in their first year has increased from 45% to 57%, and the average number of failed gateway courses per student has decreased by 24%. At the same time, the first-to-second-year retention rate at FIU has increased by 3% during the life of the G2C project, justifying confidence that the course redesign efforts contributed to this positive trajectory.

Course-specific results have been remarkable, and the largest increases in improved passing rates have been in mathematics courses. For example, in 2010, college algebra had a 30% passing/70% failing rate in its baseline year, and 23% of the first-year students who failed this course dropped out of FIU. By 2015, the college algebra passing rate had increased to 69%. Furthermore, these results led to significant cost savings in that many course sections did not need to be offered (now that more students passed rather than reenrolled in the course). More than 2,000 college algebra seats have been saved since fall 2012, equivalent to more than 50 class sections.

Together, FIU's initiatives led to student-centered active learning in redesigned gateway courses and the introduction of notable shifts in departmental practices and policies, such as the strategic scheduling of key classes. Perhaps most gratifying has been the G2C project's impact on the broader teaching and learning culture at FIU. As an institution, FIU has addressed not just evidence-informed course design but also faculty attitudes toward student learning, their responsibility for student success, and their power to bring about change. And they have risen to the task, inspiring their colleagues and creating a generative teaching culture along the way.

John N. Gardner Institute Teaching and Learning Academy. Drawing on these experiences and expertise, the authors of this article collaborated on the design and facilitation of the faculty-development process associated with the Gardner Institute's G2C program, called the Teaching and Learning Academy (TLA). TLA is a large-scale project that brings together faculty from multiple institutions to engage collaboratively in gateway-course redesign within a broad framework of understanding both the issues at stake for students and the evidence-informed strategies that enhance student learning. TLA has involved more than 230 instructors in redesigning gateway courses at 30 colleges and universities in the United States. More important, TLA serves as a catalyst for faculty, faculty developers, and academic administrators to build both effective practices and the capacity to sustain course-redesign efforts on their own campuses.

TLA consists of a daylong workshop introducing participants to evidence-informed processes to align goals to assessments and active learning activities that have been shown to improve student outcomes. TLA workshop activities include a combination of faculty-led discussions, examination of case studies (such as the previously mentioned example from URI), and individual work time. Program elements are tailored to meet the distinct needs both of faculty new to thinking about gateway-course design and of more experienced colleagues seeking to ramp up their redesign efforts. Learning from the extraordinary capacity-building efforts at FIU, TLA provides dedicated time for faculty developers and administrators to discuss their work with peers from other institutions and also to develop action plans with their own campus teams. Following the face-to-face workshop, TLA offers a yearlong program of online community and support—the TLA virtual community of practice—through webinars, biweekly newsletters featuring evidence-informed practices, and an online discussion platform. The goal of the yearlong virtual community is to provide ongoing support for applying the evidence-based pedagogies learned in the TLA workshop to instruction in gateway courses in future terms.

After three iterations of offering the TLA in 2016 and 2017, feedback from and course revisions made by participants demonstrate that gateway faculty need ongoing support to implement and sustain their plans. Faculty-development programs often focus on design—supporting faculty in developing clear course goals, related pedagogies, and specific assessment strategies. These are essential steps, but gateway-course faculty development should not stop there. Many faculty still struggle to implement their plans, to gather feedback on the results of their pedagogical changes, and to sustain the course improvement process over time.

Throughout the TLA, the most common practical concern faculty members express is: "How do I balance attention to course content with new pedagogical techniques?" Many faculty members perceive a real struggle in carving out time for students to actively participate in processing what they are learning (as research on active learning recommends). Many TLA faculty members also struggle to clearly articulate their own goals for gateway-course redesign. TLA data suggest that working with disciplinary peers is a particularly effective approach faculty can use to develop their goals and to design and implement revised course plans.

Based on these themes, the TLA design process continues to evolve to encompass evidence-informed skills and techniques that faculty need to redesign their courses in addition to supporting the development of the dispositions needed to sustain pedagogical reform across multiple terms. We believe fostering this generative culture of educational development is essential to addressing challenges faculty face in teaching and designing gateway courses.

What We Have Learned About Faculty Development for Gateway Courses

From these cases, we have identified three dispositional elements that have a powerful impact on faculty motivation and sustained engagement with gateway-course design and teaching. These attributes mirror some of the most commonly mentioned capacities that gateway-course faculty describe as important for their own students, creating a powerful resonance between the aims of faculty development and student learning.

1. Hope

> For me it is hard to understand what motivates current students. So, I am not sure whether any change will have much of an impact.
>
> **—TLA participant, 2016**

Hope can be hard to find in some gateway courses, particularly when dedicated faculty have struggled for years to improve their teaching but still witness frustratingly high failure rates. Scholars have identified the significance of *academic hope* as a foundational factor in student learning (Day, Hanson, Maltby, Proctor, & Wood, 2010; Rand, Martin, & Shea, 2011).

For instance, Julie Rattray (2016) demonstrates that students who describe themselves as "hopeful" are more likely than their peers to remain motivated in the face of difficulty in a class. This fact echoes research on faculty careers by O'Meara, Terosky, and Neumann (2008), which reveals that faculty who operate within a "narrative of growth" are more likely to be academically successful than their colleagues who describe their own work within a "narrative of constraint." Both the research on student academic hope and the scholarship of faculty career narratives also reveal that these orientations can be developed; a person can learn to become productively hopeful and to develop a growth mind-set (Dweck, 2016). Aspects of the TLA process that support faculty in feeling more hopeful include having time to articulate goals with other faculty from the same discipline and to reflect on what they already do well in their own gateway-course teaching—helping them take an assets-based approach to their redesign efforts and recognize that they are not alone in facing challenges in teaching gateway courses.

2. Agency

I am just one faculty member in a large department. Buy-in from other faculty will be necessary in order to bring about significant change at my institution overall.

—TLA participant, 2017

While a workshop might inspire hope, that alone is not enough. O'Meara, Rivera, Kuvaeva, and Corrigan (2017) highlight the importance of developing productive departmental contexts to enable faculty to adopt positive perspectives about their role in the department as well as appropriate actions they can take to increase student success. The TLA demonstrates that faculty need to see themselves as having the capacity to contribute to both student learning in their own courses and larger-scale institutional change. Once faculty have a sense that positive change is possible, as described in Professor Fournier's earlier example, they tend to experience a sense of agency—a belief that their actions matter. And empowering department chairs, as FIU has done, begins to shape the departmental context for this work. Effective gateway-course faculty development must help instructors develop the sense that they can and should act and that they know enough to make an informed attempt at improvement. One faculty member recognized this agency, inspiring her to work toward institutional change on campus:

I found the conversations with various members of the greater [TLA] community most helpful and insightful. This has inspired me to go back to my university and be more assertive with getting more faculty and graduate teaching assistants on the active learning strategies bandwagon.

—TLA participant, 2017

3. Persistence in Evidence-Informed Redesign Efforts

Implementation is usually difficult, sometimes involving several attempts to
get things right. Even when implemented well, student gains may be minimal.
—**TLA participant, 2017**

Persistence is the final essential element for both individual course design and broader cultural change to take hold. Pedagogical reforms rarely
result in quick transformations in student success; rather, the tools and processes that lead to improvements in teaching and learning typically require
time and commitment to have a significant effect. In 2017, one TLA faculty
team reported that first-semester postrevision data indicated little change in
DFWI rates. One group member declared they should *not* try active learning strategies again since their first attempt had failed; others on the team,
however, remained determined to refine their teaching and assessment. This
disappointing result is a reminder that gateway-course faculty development,
like gateway-course teaching, is not "one and done." Doing the hard work
of improving gateway courses often yields only incremental positive outcomes; the cumulative power of these small changes, however, can be significant over time (Kurtzeil & Wu, 2015). Even when reforms build on early
success, as in the G2C project at FIU, even more can be done to further enhance outcomes and sustain the gains made to date.

When hope, agency, and persistence are practiced and valued by individual faculty, in departments, and across institutions, the effect is multi-
plied; it's easier to be hopeful and to persist in a culture that nurtures these
capacities. For example, one longtime faculty member came to the 2016
TLA workshop expressing considerable doubt that he could persuade his
colleagues to change their teaching in a STEM gateway course. He told us
he valued active learning and aligned assessments, but his peers always re-
sisted any efforts at reform. In so many words, he told us he had hope for
his own class, but not for the other dozen sections of this gateway course. A
year later, his leadership had persuaded a handful of colleagues to join him
in making common revisions to improve the course's clarity, pedagogy, and
assessments—and the results in these sections demonstrated the potential
of what students could achieve in this challenging course, as failure and
withdrawal rates plunged from the historical average of roughly 50% to approximately 10% in each of the transformed sections. He and his colleagues
are hopeful that these results and their collective work will convince other
peers to join in this effort.

Conclusion

Addressing a crowd of more than 450 faculty and administrators at the
Gardner Institute's 2017 Gateway Course Experience Conference, Randy
Bass, vice provost for education at Georgetown University, underscored the

moral imperative of gateway-course redesign: "If you know it is working in other places, why aren't *you* doing it?" Just as research has demonstrated that affective elements influence student learning, we have found that in faculty development, we also need to cultivate hope, agency, and persistence in gateway-course reform initiatives. By nurturing a generative culture in gateway-course teaching and learning, faculty developers can contribute to significant, even transformational, improvements in student success.

References

Bailey, T., Jaggars, S., & Jenkins, D. (2015) *Redesigning America's community colleges.* Cambridge, MA: Harvard University Press.

Condon, W., Iverson, E. R., Manduca, C. A., Rutz, C., & Willett, G. (2016). *Faculty development and student learning: Assessing the connections.* Bloomington: Indiana University Press.

Day, L., Hanson, K., Maltby, J., Proctor, C., & Wood, A. (2010). Hope uniquely predicts objective academic achievement above intelligence, personality, and previous academic achievement. *Journal of Research in Personality, 44*(4), 550–553.

Dweck, C. (2016). *Mindset: Changing the way you think to fulfill your potential.* Updated ed. New York, NY: Ballantine/Random House.

Eagan, M. K., Jr., & Jaeger, A. J. (2008). Closing the gate: Part-time faculty instruction in gatekeeper courses and first-year persistence. In J. Braxton (Ed.), *New Directions for Teaching and Learning: No. 115. The role of the classroom in college student persistence* (pp. 39–53). San Francisco, CA: Jossey-Bass. https://doi.org/10.1002/tl.324

Evenbeck, S. E., & Jackson, B. (2005). Faculty development and the first year. In M. L. Upcraft, J. N. Gardner, B. O. Barefoot, & Associates (Eds.), *Challenging and supporting the first-year student* (pp. 257–274). San Francisco, CA: Jossey-Bass.

Fournier, K. A., Couret, J., Ramsay, J. B., & Caulkins, J. L. (2017). Using collaborative two stage examinations to address test anxiety in a large enrollment gateway course. *Anatomical Sciences Education.* https://doi.org/10.1002/ase.1677

Freeman, S., Eddy, S. L., McDonough, M., Smith, M. K., Okoroafor, N., Jordt, H., & Wenderoth, M. P. (2014). Active learning increases student performance in science, engineering, and mathematics. *Proceedings of the National Academy of Sciences, USA, 111*(23), 8410–8415.

Koch, A. K. (2017, May). Many thousands failed: A wakeup call to history educators. *Perspectives on History, 55,* 18–19. Retrieved from https://goo.gl/AiDUrB

Kurtzeil, M., & Wu, D. (2015, April 23). *Building a pathway to student success at Georgia State University.* Retrieved from https://goo.gl/wSW23T

O'Meara, K., Rivera, M., Kuvaeva, A., & Corrigan, K. (2017). Faculty learning matters: Organizational conditions and contexts that shape faculty learning. *Innovative Higher Education,* 1–22.

O'Meara, K., Terosky, A. L., & Neumann, A. (2008). Faculty careers and work lives: A professional growth perspective. *ASHE Higher Education Report, 34*(3), 1–221.

Pandey, C., & Kapitanoff, S. (2011). The influence of anxiety and quality of interaction on collaborative test performance. *Active Learning in Higher Education, 12*(3), 163–174.

Perna, L., & Jones, A. (Eds.). (2013). *The state of college access and completion: Improving college success for students from underrepresented groups.* New York, NY: Routledge.

Rand, K. L., Martin, A. D., & Shea, A. M. (2011). Hope, but not optimism, predicts academic performance of law students beyond previous academic achievement. *Journal of Research in Personality, 45*(6), 683–686.

Rattray, J. (2016). Affective dimensions of liminality. In R. Land, J. Meyer, & M. Flana-
gan (Eds.), *Threshold concepts in practice* (pp. 67–76). Rotterdam, The Netherlands:
Sense Publishers.

Stearns, S. A. (1996). Collaborative exams as learning tools. *College Teaching, 44*(3),
111–112.

SUSANNAH MCGOWAN *is a senior teaching fellow at King's College London and
a fellow at the John N. Gardner Institute for Excellence in Undergraduate Education.*

PETER FELTEN *is the assistant provost for teaching and learning, executive director of the Center for Engaged Learning, and professor of history at Elon University, and a fellow at the John N. Gardner Institute for Excellence in Undergraduate Education.*

JOSHUA CAULKINS *is the assistant director of faculty development at the University of Rhode Island and a fellow at the John N. Gardner Institute for Excellence
in Undergraduate Education.*

ISIS ARTZE-VEGA *is the assistant vice president for teaching and learning at
Florida International University and a fellow at the John N. Gardner Institute
for Excellence in Undergraduate Education.*

NEW DIRECTIONS FOR HIGHER EDUCATION • DOI: 10.1002/he

Among persistence and retention agenda initiatives undertaken by colleges and universities, gateway-course improvement efforts are often overlooked. However, the engagement of diverse institutional stakeholders in the transformation of gateway courses can contribute significantly to student success. Chief academic officers are in a unique position to sponsor such initiatives.

Chief Academic Officers and Gateway Courses: Keys to Institutional Retention and Persistence Agendas

Roberta S. Matthews, Scott Newman

As former and current chief academic officers (CAOs), we know firsthand how demanding the CAO position can be. Nevertheless, we proffer for consideration yet another major area of opportunity too often overlooked by CAOs who seek to improve the success of students at their colleges or universities: gateway courses. We strongly encourage CAOs of institutions for which gateway-course efforts are not already central to their persistence and retention strategies to investigate gateway courses further. Initiatives focused on these courses can yield important and measurable paybacks and complement a number of existing efforts to improve student success (Koch, 2012). This chapter focuses on how CAOs can help their institutions reap the benefits of gateway course–focused improvement activities.

Occurring at the very beginning of a student's tenure in higher education, gateway courses are sometimes considered less important than more advanced or major-focused course work. Gateway courses are sometimes celebrated as maintaining standards and fulfilling the important function of eliminating students who do not have the capacities to advance in a particular discipline. As central as gateway courses are to the educational endeavor, they often escape close scrutiny. However, the days of "Look to your left and look to your right—one of you will not be here by the end of this semester" are over. Allowing courses in which large percentages of students receive grades of D, F, W (withdrawal), or I (incomplete) to escape scrutiny is no longer—if it ever was—a viable option in today's higher education climate.

NEW DIRECTIONS FOR HIGHER EDUCATION, no. 180, Winter 2017   © 2017 Wiley Periodicals, Inc.
Published online in Wiley Online Library (wileyonlinelibrary.com) • DOI: 10.1002/he.20262

Gateway-Course Improvement Initiatives in Context

Higher education professionals have focused on student retention and persistence for decades, but the past few years have seen a significantly greater emphasis on these issues than any previous period. Key motivating factors for the retention and completion emphasis include institutional mission and/or values, moral imperatives concerning the waste and expense for students who depart from institutions with debt and no marketable credentials, heightened competition for new students, increased pressures by policy makers to demonstrate both institutional efficiencies and effectiveness and organizational fiscal health (Braxton et al., 2013). The institutions with which we have been affiliated have themselves undertaken numerous persistence and retention initiatives. These initiatives were generally supported by research literature, undertaken by task forces or individuals (prompted, for example, by readings or workshops), and selected and developed based on their predicted positive impacts. Through our experiences with these and other efforts, we have come to view gateway-course initiatives as essential and often missing elements in institutional persistence and retention agendas.

Identifying Allies and Leaders

In undertaking gateway-course initiatives, CAOs must, based on the size and structure of their respective institutions, first determine with whom they will work (e.g., deans, department chairs, course coordinators/lead faculty and/or other academic personnel, and, certainly, institutional research personnel) and what roles each will play. CAOs do not need to be the hands-on leaders of gateway-course reform efforts; indeed, depending on the size and culture of the institution, others might be more suited to orchestrating the operation of such initiatives. In particular, CAOs, or the individuals directly in charge of this work, should identify faculty already enjoying great success in teaching gateway courses and whose students perform well in subsequent related course work, and enlist them as allies. Multisection courses nearly always have at least one faculty member whose pass rates and students' performance in successive courses stand out as exemplary. To succeed in gateway work that will potentially include many different kinds of courses, a CAO needs to have identified personnel throughout the institution who will be committed to reviewing the data, setting goals, and collaborating across a variety of units to achieve those goals. And, most important, the CAO must initiate, orchestrate, and unequivocally support efforts to improve retention and persistence through gateway-course improvement.

Sharing Data

Many CAOs share special relationships with their offices of institutional research. Using the resources of such units to generate data about gateway courses and their effects on student persistence and retention can clarify and highlight the often negative institutional impact these courses have and galvanize faculty and staff to ensure that the improvement of gateway courses is an institutional priority. (See Chapter 3 in this volume.)

The review of data on the percentages of students receiving D, F, W, or I grades in gateway courses yields information applicable to the core work of a variety of academic personnel—including full-time and adjunct faculty, graduate students, advisors, tutors, department heads, deans, and CAOs. Analyzing student enrollment and performance data with the goal of identifying and mitigating barriers to student success in gateway-course work challenges many in higher education to think differently and develop new, important skill sets. Further, gateway-course initiatives advance the institutional culture of retention and persistence by creating greater awareness of the implications, both human and financial, of unsatisfactory student performance in entry-level courses. Too many gateway courses represent perfect storms of revolving teaching staff, inappropriate content students will never need or use in subsequent course work, and high failure or noncompletion rates among students. To the extent that general education programs include introductory courses meant to screen potential majors, the problem is exacerbated.

To fully engage a diversity of stakeholders in gateway-course efforts, CAOs will likely need to share information that is available, but frequently not shared widely among stakeholders whose actions and attitudes could be shaped by access to such information. For instance, many higher education employees have little or no idea about how budgets work. Rarely do they think of budgets as living documents they can affect through their actions. Often, when faculty are dismissed as "unrealistic," their demands stem from a lack of knowledge or from misunderstandings about budgets and other data. Faculty and staff need to understand the budgetary implications of losing students, and why, from a number of perspectives, it is incumbent upon colleges and universities, without compromising standards, to work to retain students and provide them with successful and worthwhile academic experiences.

Data should be used as a window into exploring and determining the sensible and prudent actions necessary to ensure student success. Conversations need to be facilitated regarding institutional beliefs about acceptable DFWI rates and how all members of the academic community might work together to achieve acceptable levels of student success instead of, as is too often the case, passively accepting existing levels of failure.

Another essential data point relates to addressing the "if only we had better students" argument. With regard to particular courses and majors, as well as institutionally, CAOs need to share data about what would happen to enrollments and their impacts on budgets if, for example, institutions were to raise their admissions standards or increase placement requirements. Considering the demographic, enrollment, and financial outcomes of such changes is business as usual for many in higher education administration. Too often, however, faculty and staff are unaware of the practical implications of student persistence and retention and of the "get us better students" argument.

Identifying and Reviewing Gateway Courses of All Kinds

Undertaking a review of the scope and purpose of existing gateway developmental, introductory, and general education courses is a good place to begin gateway-course review. Institutions with developmental offerings might consider linking developmental and nondevelopmental course work as intentional corequisites. Community colleges all over the United States have been creating such linkage for years. See, for example, information on the longstanding and acclaimed work of the Accelerated Learning Program (n.d.) at the Community College of Baltimore County found at http://alp-deved.org. Among others, reports from Complete College America (2012) document a variety of methods utilized in springing the developmental trap and successfully placing students into nondevelopmental course work while addressing their developmental academic needs. Many success stories regarding such efforts exist (Smith, MacGregor, Matthews, & Gabelnick, 2004).

Mathematics, a definitive gateway subject, is undergoing its own particular scrutiny focused on the kinds of mathematical knowledge and skills that are necessary and useful for students who will not be going on to calculus:

> Gateway mathematics courses should reflect students' programs of study—in many cases, that course will not be College Algebra or Precalculus. With new Math Pathways, there is no shortage of relevant mathematics, and broad consensus now exists in the American mathematics community that relevance and rigor are hallmarks of good mathematics education. (Treisman, n.d.)

One example of the attempt to bring mathematics education more in line with reality is the Math Pathways, through which Quantway, a developmental course designed to enhance quantitative literacy as the means for preparing students for college-level courses, and Statway, a course that combines college-level statistics with developmental math, were created. Both courses are designed to provide students with practical information they will actually need (Carnegie Foundation for the Advancement of Teaching, n.d.). Additional college-level math courses are being developed as well.

In some cases, institutional general education programs are filled with shortcut classes that fulfill more than one purpose (e.g., a biology course that also serves as a preparatory course for students who will take anatomy and physiology). What years ago might have seemed a prudent, fiscally wise means of creating multifunction courses has, in some instances, resulted in

NEW DIRECTIONS FOR HIGHER EDUCATION • DOI: 10.1002/he

course work that serves neither general education nor major requirements. Reviewing the purposes of general education courses may reveal courses that serve no students well. This is especially the case at institutions that offer multisection courses taught by different faculties. Such courses often confound students and contribute to high failure rates when general education students are placed in courses designed to prepare students for rigorous major course work, while students who register for a course theoretically designed to give them the necessary background and experience to thrive in disciplinary courses find themselves doing course work that does not deliver what they subsequently need to succeed.

General education and introductory major courses serve two different populations with divergent needs and expectations, and colleges and universities should, whenever possible, develop distinct courses for those groups. If the same course must serve two populations, it is incumbent upon the institution to differentiate sections meant for different kinds of students. Otherwise, such courses may run the risk of underpreparing or overwhelming students.

Deconstructing Silos

An essential component of any student persistence and retention agenda involves the building of bridges between student services and various academic areas. Such linkages help professionals of various kinds share information and together brainstorm how to best serve the students they share. Students should receive consistent and reinforcing messages about all aspects of academic life. Under the category of "Check your silos and work to break them down," CAOs can play key roles in helping connect the dots among faculty and student affairs staff and between the myriad of programs and services each provides.

There are almost as many models for advisement as there are students being advised. Nevertheless, CAOs should have a clear sense of the scope of student advisement within their institutions—to include who may be advising students at different stages in their academic careers. In most cases, common training can play a major role in ensuring that students receive consistent, accurate advisement as they work toward graduation.

In addition, CAOs should be aware of the level of coordination and communication between faculty and tutors, as well as other local support programs. Too often, there is insufficient coordination among individual departments and faculty members with any number of undergraduates, graduate students, or other adults hired to offer academic support of various kinds, in various contexts, to students. If coordination among these entities is nonexistent or low, duplication or gaps in support services may exist and signal the need for improvement. Those who serve the same students, regardless of where they are housed, how their roles are defined, or their titles, need to share information about the students regularly. Assistance

NEW DIRECTIONS FOR HIGHER EDUCATION • DOI: 10.1002/he

sessions that are well attended and well organized will have little impact on student performance if the materials covered are not closely related to what is covered in course work. Indeed, as David Arendale (2016) points out in reference to Keimig's (1983) Hierarchy of Learning Improvement Programs, "the highest level of student outcomes occurs when a comprehensive learning system is integrated throughout the course learning experience," while the lowest student outcomes are linked to efforts that are "adjunct to the course and provide support for it through either voluntary or required participation."

Colleges and universities need to avoid the proliferation of well-intentioned interventions, often at great expense, that exist apart from what is happening in particular classrooms. Large campuses too often offer a large menu of assistance venues, and students are encouraged to drop by, as if each were a different theme cafeteria whose samples one might like (or not). Such free choice offers yet another layer of confusion for first-year students, who often have difficulty locating and navigating new spaces and rarely seek help on their own until whatever intervention occurs, and whatever its quality, occurs way too late to make a difference.

Faculty teaching a course, advisors working with students in the course, and tutors and others helping those students all need to know what is happening in each venue. The bar for coordination and communication among them must be set high, far above merely encouraging attendance or suggesting or writing referrals. Tutors and other support personnel often have clear ideas about the best way they can serve students, and it behooves faculty and academic leaders to give them a voice, integrate them into course planning, and act on their suggestions.

Outreach to Students

As Andrew Koch notes in Chapter 1 of this volume, in many colleges and universities the chances are great that large percentages of incoming students are the first in their families to attend institutions of higher learning. Institutions that have not already collected data on first-generation students should do so. That first-generation students are among the most at risk in higher education is now well understood (Opidee, 2015; Pappano, 2015). Therefore, academic and student-services staff members at colleges and universities with large numbers of first-generation students will need to work together to develop targeted programs that address their needs (Strand, 2013).

Just as higher education institutions should direct special efforts to the needs of first-generation students, they can also enlist high-performing and upper-division students in supporting their younger, less experienced peers. Institutions should brainstorm how to use their best students as well as solicit students' ideas about how they might help their peers. Strong students are often willing, if not eager, to share their strategies for success with students who could benefit from such insights. In many cases, honors students are required to perform some form of community service. At Brooklyn College of the City University of New York, as an option for community service, a dean in the Office for Undergraduate Studies facilitated meetings between honors students and low-performing students so that the high achievers could share how they studied and tackled academic problems. Typically, in such cases, both sets of students enjoy such encounters with each other, and less strong students benefit from their stronger peers' helpful advice and tips.

Linking strong and less strong students in other ways can also yield positive outcomes. Formal programs such as supplemental instruction (Martin & Arendale, 1994) help colleges and universities establish ongoing training sessions in which high-performing students offer integrated, formal, ongoing support to students in select courses. The groundbreaking work by Martin and Arendale set the standard for effective and carefully targeted use of students in classrooms. As well, student tutors often have concrete and clear ideas about how to best reinforce classroom learning. Generally, reaching out and listening to students who are in positions to help their peers through their perspectives and suggestions can enrich institutional gateway-course efforts.

Finally, and most important, engaging faculty in the transformation of their own courses is both the primary key and challenge of examining and improving gateway courses (Ambrose, Bridges, DiPietro, Lovett & Norman, 2010). With regard to first-year gateway-course work, James Slevin, a former department chair at Georgetown University who is an expert in composition, theories of literacy, and community-based intellectual work, aptly captures the issue at the center of this type of course reform. During a speech to the Modern Language Association, Slevin (2005), in response to a colleague's suggestion that developmental and major course work should be separate, asserted that every introductory course "must be seen as radically remedial in both its purposes and pedagogies. . . . [No] student is really prepared for it, which is precisely why it is important. Where the course is not conceivable as remedial, it needs to be rethought to make it so." Most new students do not know how to be college students, and too many learn through experience that approaching their postsecondary studies as a high school student is a likely recipe for failure.

Honoring Those Who Teach While Supporting and Enriching Their Efforts

In large research universities, where teaching may play a less central role than on other campuses, CAOs must often make the case for the importance of focusing on good teaching and support their words with actions that acknowledge and promote good teaching in critical reappointment, promotion, and tenure contexts and in palpable awards for such important work (Hutchings, Huber, & Ciccone, 2011). Often this requires a serious reconsideration and realignment of institutional priorities on the part of deans, chairpersons, and faculty themselves. Conversations need to occur in which all involved air their priorities, values, and hopes for their students and the contributions they will make to society. Further, CAOs can help create and, if they already exist, support environments that honor teaching and insist that faculty learn and apply the often simple (rarely time-consuming), proven, and documented approaches that contribute to student success.

In all institutions, CAOs need to acknowledge the realities of teaching large course sections with many students and encourage campus centers for teaching and learning (CTLs) to facilitate targeted, disciplinary-based workshops for specific courses and disciplines. Too often, the services of such centers are underutilized and lack the kind of cooperation from deans and department chairs that maximizes the effectiveness of CTLs. Excellent, research-based, discipline-focused material on teaching and learning is readily available (Wiggins & McTighe, 2005); a lack of awareness of the extensive body of work available on how students learn is no longer a tenable posture. The scholarship of teaching is alive and well, and CAOs should facilitate its introduction on their campuses. They must overtly support those faculty who are already applying this important scholarship to their teaching and must work with CTLs to offer targeted and effective faculty development workshops that speak to the expressed, diverse needs of faculty members who are teaching gateway courses.

The Role of Disciplinary Organizations

As Brookins and Swafford make clear in Chapter 7 in this volume, higher education disciplinary organizations can be important resources for CAOs committed to improving persistence and success in gateway courses. Virtually all such organizations, across the diversity of academic disciplines, have developed course objectives and student outcomes for the most basic and universal courses in the curriculum, and frequently have experimented with and promoted relevant innovative pedagogies. The websites of disciplinary organizations can be invaluable sources of information that address faculty members in their disciplinary languages.

CAO Roundup of Roles

As noted earlier, CAOs occupy positions widely regarded as among the most challenging in higher education—in no small part because they bear significant responsibilities for the success of their institutions' persistence and retention agendas. The following recommendations focus on the specific, important roles that CAOs can fulfill with respect to their institutions' persistence and retention agendas in general and gateway-course initiatives in particular. CAOs should:

NEW DIRECTIONS FOR HIGHER EDUCATION • DOI: 10.1002/he

- *Provide focus in the noise.* Given the volume of information about student success agendas, CAOs can play important roles by helping prioritize, by assessing the time and costs involved, and by lending focus to such initiatives.
- *Ensure inclusion of appropriate constituencies.* CAOs have the broad perspectives to identify and engage a diversity of institutional stakeholders who may hold valuable insights and/or contribute to initiatives in unique ways. CAOs help ensure that the right individuals are engaged.
- *Align interests, capacities, and initiatives.* CAOs can assist in identifying potential alignments and promoting synergies among individuals and units engaged in various persistence and retention efforts.
- *Keep persistence and retention activities complementary.* CAOs are in a unique position and have the broad perspective to avoid duplication of efforts. They can ensure a more effective use of college and university resources.
- *Champion institutional persistence and retention initiatives.* CAOs can use their offices to keep key institutional priorities and related resource allocation at the forefront of the minds of institutional stakeholders.
- *Lend structure and accountability to student success activities.* CAOs commonly play important roles in establishing major benchmarks, time lines, and deliverables, as well as ensuring that those engaged are accountable for stated outcomes.
- *Ensure alignment between institutional efforts oriented toward student success.* CAOs can help ensure related initiatives are appropriate to their institutions and the students they serve (Kuh, 2003, 2008).
- *Keep student success efforts focused on the institution.* Far too many dialogues on college and university campuses degenerate into unconstructive gripe sessions that blame students, parents, secondary education, and society. CAOs can help institutions focus on their role in improving the success of their students.
- *Help manage retention and persistence fatigue.* CAOs can assist by prioritizing which initiatives are undertaken when, as well as ensuring that the responsibilities for such activities do not always fall to a single unit or small group of individuals.
- *Link the improvement of teaching and learning to positive changes in student retention and persistence* to underscore the close relationship between them (Bain, 2011).

CAOs fulfill unique roles within their institutions. They owe it to their colleges and universities, and to the students and communities they serve, to take strong positions with respect to gateway-course initiatives. The persistence and retention of students depend on CAO involvement in and support of this important work.

References

Accelerated Learning Program. (n.d.). Retrieved from http://alp-deved.org/

Ambrose, S. A., Bridges, M. W., DiPietro, M., Lovett, M. C., & Norman, M. K. (2010). *How learning works: Seven research-based principles for smart teaching.* San Francisco, CA: Jossey-Bass.

Arendale, D. (2016). *Postsecondary peer cooperative learning programs: Annotated bibliography.* Minneapolis: University of Minnesota. Updated versions of this document available at http://z.umn.edu/peerbib

Bain, K. (2011). *What the best college teachers do.* Cambridge, MA: Harvard University Press.

Braxton, J. M., Doyle, W. R., Hartley, H. V., III, Hirschy, A. S., Jones, W. A., & McLendon, M. K. (2013). *Rethinking college student retention.* San Francisco, CA: Jossey-Bass.

Carnegie Foundation for the Advancement of Teaching. (n.d.). *Carnegie math pathways.* Retrieved from https://www.carnegiefoundation.org/in-action/carnegie-math-pathways

Complete College America. (2012). *Remediation: Higher education's bridge to nowhere.* Retrieved from http://www.completecollege.org/docs/CCA-Remediation-final.pdf/

Hutchings, P., Huber, M. T., & Ciccone, A. (2011). *The scholarship of teaching and learning reconsidered: Institutional integration and impact.* San Francisco, CA: Jossey-Bass.

Keimig, R. T. (1983). *Raising academic standards: A guide to learning improvement.* ASHE-ERIC Higher Education Research Report, No. 4. Washington, DC: Association for the Study of Higher Education, ERIC Clearinghouse on Higher Education.

Koch, A. K. (2012). A call to action: Why high enrollment, high-risk, gateway courses require an intentional institutional improvement effort. In M. D. Pistilli (Ed.), *Using analytics to create real solutions for real problems: Essays and reflections from the SoLAR Flare practitioner's conference at Purdue University* (pp. 27–44). Retrieved from https://solaresearch.org/wp-content/uploads/2012/06/PurdueSolarFlareCompliation v1.pdf

Kuh, G. D. (2003). What we're learning about student engagement. *Change, 35*(2), 24–32.

Kuh, G. D. (2008). *High impact educational practices: What they are, who has access to them, and why they matter.* Washington, DC: Association of American Colleges & Universities.

Martin, D. C., & Arendale, D. (Eds.). (1994). *Supplemental instruction: Increasing achievement and retention.* San Francisco, CA: Jossey-Bass.

Opidee, I. (2015). Supporting first-gen college students. *University Business, 18*(3), 32–36. Retrieved from https://www.universitybusiness.com/article/supporting-first-gen-college-students/

Pappano, L. (2015, April 8). *First-generation students unite.* Retrieved from http://www.nytimes.com/2015/04/12/education/edlife/first-generation-students-unite .html/

Slevin, J. F. (2005). Association of Departments of English, Francis Andrew March Award for Distinguished Service to the Profession of English. Address presented at the Modern Language Association Annual Convention, Washington, DC.

Smith, B., MacGregor, J., Matthews, R., & Gabelnick, F. (2004). *Learning communities: Reforming undergraduate education.* San Francisco, CA: Jossey-Bass.

Strand, K. J. (2013). *Making sure they make it! Best practices for ensuring the academic success of first-generation college students.* Washington, DC: Council of Independent Colleges/Walmart Foundation.

Treisman, Uri. (n.d.). *Game changers: Math pathways*. Complete College America. Retrieved from http://completecollege.org/

Wiggins, G., & McTighe, J. (2005). *Understanding by design* (2nd ed.). Alexandria, VA: ASCD.

ROBERTA S. MATTHEWS served as the associate dean of faculty, acting dean, and acting president at LaGuardia Community College (CUNY); vice president for academic affairs at Marymount College, Tarrytown, NY; and provost of Brooklyn College (CUNY). She is currently a senior fellow at the John N. Gardner Institute for Excellence in Undergraduate Education.

SCOTT NEWMAN is vice president of academic affairs at the Oklahoma State University Institute of Technology.

7

Academic faculty members often maintain strong identities based on the primary discipline of their graduate training and teaching. While teaching cultures differ across fields, disciplinary associations like the American Historical Association have been active in supporting student-centered curricular work.

Why Gateway-Course Improvement Should Matter to Academic Discipline Associations and What They Can Do to Address the Issues

Julia Brookins, Emily Swafford

As the oldest and largest disciplinary organization in the United States for historians, the American Historical Association (AHA) has been leading wide-ranging considerations of the connections among disciplinary learning in history, professional preparation for teaching, and the role of historical thinking in public culture. While these efforts take numerous forms in terms of initiatives, programming, and publications, improving gateway education has emerged as a key arena for tackling a number of critical member concerns and for communicating effectively with a variety of external audiences. The issues and tensions surrounding gateway history courses have become an important nexus for discussion, debate, advocacy, and reform within and beyond the AHA. While this chapter focuses on the specific case of history as a discipline, it offers possible lessons for other disciplinary communities as well as for higher education leaders trying to make progress in institution, system-wide, or interdisciplinary contexts.

The Disciplinary Element in Gateway Education

What can a disciplinary focus add to a conversation about learning in general education and especially gateway courses? Based on the recent experience of the AHA, attention to the specifics of a disciplinary culture and active engagement of a discipline society in work on curricular and teaching projects show promise in catalyzing and sustaining faculty

NEW DIRECTIONS FOR HIGHER EDUCATION, no. 180, Winter 2017 © 2017 Wiley Periodicals, Inc.
Published online in Wiley Online Library (wileyonlinelibrary.com) • DOI: 10.1002/he.20263

engagement to improve student success. Discipline-based scholarly societies enjoy significant professional legitimacy among higher education faculty members. These organizations are well positioned to convene practitioners and implement processes that provide instructors from a wide range of institutional types with a sense of common cause and the opportunity to pursue positive change in concert with their shared values. The disciplinary focus and deep training of faculty need not be obstacles to improving student learning in gateway courses. Indeed, they are strong and underutilized levers for reform in higher education today.

Discipline societies may be viewed as culturally authoritative but non-threatening by many postsecondary instructors in a given field. Association members who follow news and networks related to teaching and learning in their field may feel that their home association is a more trustworthy clearinghouse and a more neutral judge of the significance of certain developments in higher education for their own teaching than are local administrators, system officials, or public political institutions. Being aware of campus power dynamics and careful about taking unnecessary professional risks, they may feel that they have nothing to lose and more to gain by participating in professional development and other programming through their disciplinary association than through administratively defined channels in their home institutions.

Faculty participants in the AHA's largest teaching and curricular project over the past 4 years reported feeling reinvigorated and energized to innovate in their classrooms with the encouragement or authorization of the association. These outcomes for faculty contrasted with the perceptions of isolation and beleaguerment under external pressures that motivated many to apply for the project in the first place.

While many gateway courses are part of general education curricula, the stakes for improving student learning in gateway courses are nevertheless high for disciplinary faculty and for disciplinary associations like the AHA. In today's climate, historians need to demonstrate what we are contributing and can contribute to the entire undergraduate curriculum. The best opportunities to do that lie in gateway courses. It is in these courses that we interact with the most students. We need to make sure that students of history learn skills, knowledge, and habits of mind that facilitate their transition to college and enhance their success throughout college and after graduation. The best opportunities to demonstrate that on a large scale are in gateway courses. To the extent that any discipline's foundational course offerings are high-enrollment and high-stakes, that discipline is going to suffer the stigma of being a barrier to college success for some students. Students will also avoid those courses if possible, and institutions seeking to maximize retention and completion will have an incentive to design general education programs that bypass them. Historians have a lot to lose, as do others. In history, our departments will lose enrollments as an important recruiting stream for upper-division courses, and the number of majors will likely shrink. Importantly, the discipline will lose a chance to show a broad array of fellow citizens and voters the value of what we do.

In this chapter, using the AHA as a case study, we will explore the discipline society and the role it can play in improving student learning in gateway courses. We discuss the AHA's recent Tuning project for history, which engaged history faculty in a nationwide project to reconsider our program curricula based on what students should understand, know, and be able to do at the completion of a degree (American Historical Association, 2016). This process brought the importance of gateway courses into new focus for many participating history instructors. We provide context on how beginning history courses at the college level have long been used to fulfill several purposes—including building analytical skills, communication skills, and civic competencies—that make them critical contributors to successful college transition and college completion. We conclude that engaging discipline societies can help empower faculty to revisit the particular purposes of their own gateway courses and to innovate in their classrooms with an eye toward making those courses work better for learners.

The AHA's Interests in History Teaching

The AHA is the largest professional organization of historians, with about 12,000 members from all fields of history. Its Teaching Division is one of three divisions on its governing council and is concerned with teaching at all levels, from K–12 to doctoral education. As a membership organization and disciplinary society, the AHA seeks both to respond to and advocate for the needs of its members and to prepare for and address the anticipated needs of the future of the discipline. The AHA is not the only disciplinary association for historians—they proliferate across the many times, spaces, and themes that historians study—but it is the largest and is open to all historians within the United States. As such, it sets the standards for the research, teaching, and professional life of the discipline (American Historical Association, 2017).

Since the inception of the AHA, supporting history faculty and enabling student access to the benefits of studying history have both been at the center of its values and mission. Increasingly, the AHA fulfills this aspect of its mission by supporting faculty engagement in student learning in general education. It is not news that the landscape of higher education has undergone rapid and fundamental change in the past several decades. Many factors, from decreasing public funding of universities to fundamental shifts in who pursues a college degree and how students pay for their degrees, have contributed to a changed public understanding of the purpose and value of higher education. Within this context, enrollments in history courses and the numbers of students majoring in history are in decline. Though there are glimpses of isolated departments bucking the trends, the numbers overall are decreasing, as they are for many humanities disciplines (Brookins, 2016a, 2016b). If the AHA is to address the changing landscape and to support faculty as they address declining enrollments and majors, it is imperative for the discipline to pay attention to the role of history education in general education. Gateway courses frequently represent the only chance departments have to communicate the value of history learning to undergraduate students and, through them, to the broader stakeholders in higher education.

The role of history in general education has traditionally been defined as necessary to preparing students for active and engaged citizenship. The contest over how this ought to be accomplished is most frequently undertaken at the kindergarten through 12th-grade level, as recent debates over new frameworks released by the College Board for its advanced-placement U.S. history courses clearly illustrate (Kamenetz, 2015). Within an undergraduate general education curriculum, the most frequent parallel is that history courses are part of a "multicultural" or "global citizen" requirement. Any historian would certainly argue that the study of history fundamentally supports active and engaged citizenry, whether locally or globally. But both of these cases rely on a flat understanding of history as content, as facts or knowledge that can be statically transferred from teacher to student, a definition of history quite foreign to historians.

Most historians would agree that history is much more dynamic, and certainly more than a flat recitation of "what actually happened." But if history is more than content, then what is it? How is it defined, and who gets to define it? On this, historians are more likely to diverge, and the debate within undergraduate history education has centered on exactly this question. For the past decade or so, there has been increasing attention paid within the discipline of history to the growing body of the scholarship of teaching and learning. What are the cognitive moves that historians take for granted in doing historical analysis, how are they best taught to students, and how can student learning of these moves be assessed (Calder & Steffes, 2016; Pace, 2004; Wineburg, 2001)? The debate is hardly a settled one, but it is central to safeguarding the future of the discipline.

In history, therefore, the stakes of gateway courses and the mission of the AHA to advance the teaching and learning of history overlap. If historians are to make the case that history is more than just facts, that there are historical thinking skills that not only are important to engaged citizenry but that also enhance the pursuit of a degree in higher education, they must take seriously research on student learning. Given these ongoing debates within the discipline of history and within the larger public, both about what students of history should learn and how they should learn it, the decline in enrollments and majors within undergraduate history provides a sober reminder of the need for the discipline to reintroduce itself to students, parents, and higher education leaders and to revise its approaches to align with the needs of twenty-first-century learners and learning.

The AHA's Tuning Project and Its Implications for Gateway Courses

In the fall of 2011, the AHA received a multiyear grant from the Lumina Foundation to pursue something called "Tuning," which had evolved from the European Bologna Process and been adapted for U.S. higher education (McInerney, 2016a). The first phase of the AHA's Tuning project (2012–2015) brought together individual faculty members from more than 60 2- and 4-year colleges and universities across the United States to articulate what a student should understand, know, and be able to do at the successful completion of a history degree program. Project staff started by asking participants to reflect on what they most valued about the history discipline and to describe the outcomes that were essential to learning in the field. As a faculty-led process, the Tuning process then tasked participants with taking the shared history "discipline core" statement and using it to perform a collaborative examination of the distinctive characteristics and missions of their programs and institutions, centered on the student experience. Faculty tuners then drafted local program descriptions that were aligned to their courses and curricula and written in common language for prospective students, parents, and potential employers of graduates, among other audiences.

The second phase (2015) introduced a new group of 98 faculty from more than 60 additional institutions to the Tuning process and goals, and each individual or institutional team wrote a plan for what aspect of their programs they would work on. Some chose to revamp major requirements, to write new program learning outcomes, to work more closely with contingent faculty who taught many of their program courses, or to develop new assessment plans. Others incorporated extensive work on introductory courses. From the beginning of the project, AHA members wondered why the project focused on the major, and they suggested that service teaching of introductory courses was more important (Keeling, 2013). Indeed, reconsideration of gateway education has been the key to progress on a number of campuses (Carey, Cooper, Herbin-Triant, Misevich, & Quintana, 2013; McInerney, 2016b).

Based on the reports of external project evaluator and consultant Robert Stein, former Missouri commissioner of higher education, the overwhelming majority of individual participants did revise their own courses and try new teaching practices, although they experienced varied success in moving their departments and colleagues toward shared expressions of the purposes or outcomes of their degree programs. Many also became aware of the scholarship of teaching and learning in history and started to apply the animating questions and lessons of that nascent literature to their own pedagogies.

Tuning also gave many 4-year faculty participants and the project staff the opportunity to work closely with participating historians based at 2-year colleges. Conversations between 2- and 4-year instructors were especially important in bringing issues of students' transition to college-level work out in the open. It became clear that transparency in learning expectations between lower-division, general education courses and more advanced courses in the major was an important but neglected area for faculty collaboration between institutions.

In addition to the benefits of working across institutions through a national organization like the AHA, participants drew valuable experience from conversations among their department colleagues. Collegial departments where at least a subset of faculty members was open to thinking holistically about the program curriculum often accomplished internal reforms that were then recognized by local administrators. Many faculty members are in general only dimly aware of how teaching and learning programs in their national disciplinary communities could be brought to bear on specific campus initiatives or even for the work of reaffirmation of accreditation. The Tuning process helped some departments figure out ways to get more involved in other campus initiatives—ways that served their own needs as well as those of the institution as a whole. A number of Tuning participants and their colleagues found that, by pursuing the collaborative, faculty-led, and student-centered work of curriculum review and revision, they came to be recognized by their administrations as a leading group on campus. Some were subsequently solicited by upper administrators to share their work with other faculty and academic units as a model.

AHA staff members and elected representatives of the organization's Teaching Division did not realize at the start of the Tuning project that pursuing the grant activities would lead the organization to uncover previously unrecognized needs and constituencies, as well as new strategies for engaging those new constituencies and new approaches to meeting their needs. In short, the AHA's Tuning project helped the organization better see the needs of faculty members—especially those at nonelite colleges and universities—in the rapidly changing landscape of American higher education. And although the AHA's grant was awarded to focus on clarifying and articulating the purposes and outcomes of the history major, the subject of gateway education kept coming up and became central to many faculty participants' thinking and work on their curricula. Indeed, since the beginning of the AHA project, the Tuning process has also been paired with the work of the Association of American Colleges and Universities and the National Institute for Learning Outcomes Assessment on the Degree Qualifications Profile, an effort to define outcomes for an entire degree, including general education, cocurricular, and other learning experiences (Jankowski & Marshall, 2015).

What Is a Gateway Course in History?

Few history faculty members use the term *gateway course* in discussions about their gateway courses. Most commonly, history instructors refer to their "survey" courses or, somewhat more broadly, "introductory" courses. Even without using the term *gateway*, however, many historians have put a great deal of effort into thinking about history courses that are foundational, high-enrollment, and high-stakes. There is well over a century of literature on the forms and functions of beginning college history courses, as historians David Voelker and Joel Sipress reviewed in a 2011 *Journal of American History* article, "The End of the History Survey Course" (Sipress & Voelker, 2011). With some translation and encouragement from disciplinary leaders like those recognized in scholarly associations, the expanding efforts to improve gateway courses across disciplines can now also begin to enrich and deepen the long-standing conversations about such courses within a discipline like history. Efforts by organizations like the John N. Gardner Institute for Excellence in Undergraduate Education have the potential to connect discipline-focused instructors to valuable new ideas, allies, and resources for improving student learning.

For the discipline of history, a survey course traditionally connotes a fast sweep across a broad swath of historical time, events, and characters, often delivered through large lectures, sometimes—depending on the instructional norms of an institution—with auxiliary discussion sections where more active learning might take place. In conversation, an instructor might use the term *survey* without reflection, even when an inquiry-driven approach focusing on skills may be the goal. While a growing number of instructors experiment with course designs that are not defined exclusively by the content covered and have certain carefully articulated, skills-based learning goals, the term *survey* remains the common name historians use to talk about the category of courses that could also be called gateway courses. The more neutral term *introductory course*, which may encompass any type of format, content, or pedagogical approach at the beginning level, is nevertheless often used interchangeably with *survey*.

To the extent that history faculty may be aware of and use the term *gateway course* or *gateway learning*, the term might be confined to use within the history degree program. As one faculty member explained, he and his colleagues would be familiar with the phrase *gateway course* as a course, possibly at the sophomore level, that serves as the entry point to the history major. While such courses might still fit within the parameters of the definition of a gateway course in this volume, they do not affect as many students as the survey or introductory courses in general education. After all, while some states require a history course (or even two) for all bachelor's degree recipients, less than 2% of all U.S. bachelor's degrees are awarded to history majors (Brookins, 2016a).

Disciplinary faculty members do not always have the same definition of a gateway course, but many would share the goal of transforming obstacles to achieve greater equity and facilitate their students' transition to college learning. Most history instructors on the AHA's Tuning project have jumped at the chance to rework the introductory courses using new insights gained during their conversations with experienced peers and their independent explorations of teaching and learning literature.

Purposes of Beginning College History Courses Then and Now

In spite of the traditional terminology, many college history teachers have been making changes to the ways they teach beginning students. Increasingly, thoughtful instructors from a wide array of colleges and universities have joined scholars of teaching and learning in history in shifting the focus from teaching undergraduates *about* history to teaching them how to *do* history.

A long-running debate about the purposes of college history education, particularly the purposes of introductory history courses for nonmajors, is sometimes oversimplified into a debate between those who prioritize teaching content coverage and those who prioritize teaching skills. Most acknowledge, however, that one cannot learn skills without practicing them on particular content, and learning content without skills—whether analytical, research, interpretive, communication, or other skills—is not meaningful in and of itself. But what is the appropriate balance for particular learning levels and specific courses? Historians and others have also sought another important learning outcome in prescribing gateway history courses: civic education or preparation for citizenship. But exactly how does studying history produce better citizens?

At certain moments in American history, the dominant argument has been that every citizen must know certain things and demonstrate familiarity with key names and events or be exposed to key cases of social change; at other moments, the idea has been to train students in critical thinking to enable them to engage effectively with issues and be lifelong learners. For a review of these debates, see Sipress and Voelker (2011); for more on how historians have approached these questions, see Calder and Steffes (2016). Most recently, with the deluge of information online and elsewhere, prominent researchers in the field of history teaching and learning have emphasized that history can and should teach students how to think historically—that is, to question, check sources, and contextualize information before drawing conclusions (Wineburg, 2016). The local context for any particular gateway history course should be taken into account when considering how instructors can try to balance the content, skills, and civic goals that students, institutions, and the public have for the course. Using history as an example, it is clear that a disciplinary society has a role to play in convening instructors and supporting their exploration of possibilities to design gateway experiences that are suited to the context and students.

Conclusion: Mobilizing Faculty Members' Disciplinary Identities to Improve Learning in Gateway Courses

Working with disciplinary associations is a promising new direction in higher education. Based on the recent experiences of the AHA, particularly with its Tuning project for history, disciplinary associations have the potential to enhance and even transform faculty engagement with higher education reform. With a broad mission and clear commitment to faculty-led curricular improvement in their fields, organizations like the AHA can convene instructors nationwide, or even internationally, to share expertise and experiences to make significant progress, at scale, on some of the difficult challenges. Although still in its formative phases, work between the AHA and the Gardner Institute has the potential to connect well-intentioned and thoughtful historians with evidence to motivate changes in gateway history courses and to point them toward resources and approaches to try.

At the local level, we recommend that 2- and 4-year institutions encourage and support more academic faculty members to engage closely with relevant disciplinary associations that have an active agenda for improving teaching and learning at the undergraduate level. This might include encouraging faculty to implement a collaborative process of reflection on their own goals, providing a forum for sharing curricular and pedagogical work, and physical spaces and time for experimentation. To foster a sense of community and build momentum, administrators can provide support for professional development opportunities that are tailored to faculty needs, including discipline-specific professional development conferences and workshops. Many instructors are less motivated to engage fully in one-size-fits-all campus initiatives that seem to have limited relevance to individual courses. We also encourage educational systems and funding organizations to seek partnerships with disciplinary associations in developing and implementing reforms to general education and developmental learning, as well as in pursuing improvements in college access, student transition, and retention or graduation initiatives.

Disciplinary associations like the AHA could play a larger role in the future to make clear to individual instructors the high stakes for equity and promise in gateway education. They are positioned to do this in a community venue where instructors feel supported, not isolated and threatened. The AHA is currently building on its Tuning and other teaching and learning programs to communicate not just the need for change to eliminate barriers, particularly for minority, first-generation, and less prepared college students, but also the positive case for why historians should want to transform those barriers to achieve greater equity through better learning. This case differs sharply from the ones that some faculty perceive coming from local administrative offices or political bodies, where there is great suspicion that the means to better retention include shifting metrics, ill-conceived accountability schemes, or undercutting of shared values for intellectual rigor and genuine student achievement.

Finally, we encourage more discipline associations to take a close look at gateway-course improvement for their own sustainability. For history and other disciplines, gateway education reform can be a critical site for reaching new groups of faculty and an opportunity to learn more deeply about how external, public, and administrative concerns affect their core academic constituencies in ways that pose serious risk to the relevance and very viability of such associations in the future.

References

American Historical Association (AHA). (2016). *AHA history Tuning project: 2016 history discipline core.* Retrieved from https://www.historians.org/teaching-and-learning/tuning-the-history-discipline/2016-history-discipline-core

American Historical Association (AHA). (2017). Membership. Retrieved from https://www.historians.org/about-aha-and-membership/membership

Brookins, J. (2016a, March). New data show large drop in history bachelor's degrees. *Perspectives on History*, 10–11.

Brookins, J. (2016b, September). Survey finds fewer students enrolling in college history courses. *Perspectives on History*. Retrieved from https://www.historians.org/publications-and-directories/perspectives-on-history/september-2016/survey-finds-fewer-students-enrolling-in-college-history-courses

Calder, L., & Steffes, T. (2016). Measuring college learning in history. In R. Arum, J. Roksa, & A. Cook (Eds.), *Improving quality in American higher education: Learning outcomes and assessments for the 21st century* (pp. 7–86). San Francisco, CA: Jossey-Bass.

Carey, E., Cooper, T. A., Herbin-Triant, E., Misevich, P., & Quintana, A. (2013, April). Tuning the core: History, assessment, and the St. John's university core curriculum. *Perspectives on History*. Retrieved from https://www.historians.org/Perspectives/issues/2013/1304/Tuning-the-Core.cfm

Jankowski, N., & Marshall, D. (2015). Degree Qualifications Profile (DQP) and Tuning: What are they and why do they matter? In N. Jankowski & D. Marshall (Eds.), *New Directions for Institutional Research: No. 165. Partners in advancing student learning: Degree Qualifications Profile and Tuning* (pp. 3–13). San Francisco, CA: Jossey-Bass. https://doi.org/10.1002/ir.20120

Kamenetz, A. (2015, August 5). The new, new framework for AP U.S. history. *Morning Edition*. Retrieved from http://www.npr.org/sections/ed/2015/08/05/429361628/the-new-new-framework-for-ap-u-s-history

Keeling, D. (2013, September). On history for non-majors. *Perspectives on History*. Retrieved from http://www.historians.org/publications-and-directories/perspectives-on-history/september-2013/letter-to-the-editor-on-history-for-non-majors

McInerney, D. (2016a). The American Historical Association's Tuning project: An introduction. *History Teacher, 49*, 491–501.

McInerney, D. (2016b). The intro course as an introduction to curriculum change. *World History Connected, 13*(2). Retrieved from http://worldhistoryconnected.press.illinois.edu/13.2/forum_mcinerney.html

Pace, D. (2004, October). The amateur in the operating room: History and the scholarship of teaching and learning. *American Historical Review, 109*, 1171–1192.

Sipress, J. M., & Voelker, D. J. (2011, March). The end of the history survey course: The rise and fall of the coverage model. *Journal of American History*, 97, 1050–1066. https://doi.org/10.1093/jahist/jaq035

Wineburg, S. (2001). *Thinking historically and other unnatural acts: Charting the future of teaching the past.* Philadelphia, PA: Temple University Press.

Wineburg, S. (2016, April). Why historical thinking is not about history. *History News*, 71(2), 13–16. Retrieved from https://purl.stanford.edu/yy383km0067

JULIA BROOKINS is special projects coordinator at the American Historical Association and directed the AHA's Tuning project.

EMILY SWAFFORD is manager of academic affairs at the American Historical Association.

PART IV. INTEGRATED APPROACHES AND SYSTEMS

This part includes chapters that describe how institutions can combine various student success efforts with their gateway-course improvement strategies to increase the likelihood that the strategies are more successful and serve larger numbers of students.

8

Offered as a case study, this chapter shows how Lansing Community College intentionally combined efforts to redesign eight high-risk courses with efforts to create clearer guided curricular pathways for the college's students.

Intentionally Linking Gateway-Course Transformation Efforts with Guided Pathways

Martine Courant Rife, Christine Conner

In an effort to improve student outcomes, postsecondary institutions across the United States often find themselves involved in an array of student retention and success efforts. These programs frequently occur in disjointed ways that can, if not addressed, result in duplication of effort, missed opportunities for shared resources, and initiative fatigue. In an effort to avoid these common issues, faculty and staff from Lansing Community College (LCC) in Michigan worked to combine two student success-related efforts: a gateway-course redesign project and a separate process to design "guided pathways," in order to limit and focus the curriculum. We engaged in these efforts because we believed that doing so would make the ultimate outcomes better for all involved parties—particularly the LCC students.

According to the Community College Research Center at Columbia University, the term *pathways* has come to be used to describe "a clear road map of the courses" that students "need to take to complete a credential" and the intentional provision of "guidance and support to help (students) stay on plan" (Community College Research Center, 2015). Pathways, or Guided Pathways, are employed by many 2-year institutions, but they are also becoming a part of broader student success efforts at 4-year colleges and universities in the United States (Hopkins, 2017).

The work to transform five gateway courses at LCC began in fall 2013 when the college joined the Gateways to Completion (G2C) process directed by the John N. Gardner Institute for Excellence in Undergraduate Education (Gardner Institute). Our efforts to transform both teaching and learning in gateway courses helped us to identify larger issues affecting the performance of students. It became apparent to faculty and staff engaged

NEW DIRECTIONS FOR HIGHER EDUCATION, no. 180, Winter 2017   © 2017 Wiley Periodicals, Inc.
Published online in Wiley Online Library (wileyonlinelibrary.com) • DOI: 10.1002/he.20264

in the G2C self-study process that gateway courses existed within one or more curricular pathways that were not clearly understood by students or even faculty and staff. Jenkins (2014) succinctly describes the problem that underlies the work on pathways: "In most community colleges … many students do not see a clear path to their end goals, become frustrated, and drop out" (p. 1; see also Bailey, Jaggars, & Jenkins, 2015b).

In December 2014, LCC made a decision to join other Michigan community colleges to establish Guided Pathways for its students. Through interacting and learning from other Michigan colleges in a 2015 Michigan Guided Pathways Institute and making use of a Guided Pathways Resource Repository maintained since 2014 by the Michigan Community College Association (MCCA) (2017), LCC established a process to create clearer pathways that ultimately yielded higher levels of completion and more appropriate credentials for students. The kinds of questions LCC faculty and staff were being asked to consider by the Gardner Institute in the G2C course-transformation process meshed very well with the questions being addressed by the pathways projects administered by the MCCA and also the American Association of Community Colleges (AACC) (For more information on AACC Pathways, see   http://www.aacc.nche.edu/Resources/aaccprograms/pathways/Pages/default.aspx). It became apparent that sound pathways through higher education do not exist if students are not successfully completing gateway courses that are part of the pathways. Further, LCC faculty noted that gateway-course outcomes could be enhanced if the courses were contextualized within broader, intentionally supportive pathways. In other words, better outcomes could be achieved by linking the work on gateway courses to the Guided Pathways efforts.

Gateways to Completion (G2C)

The G2C process is "designed to create and implement an evidence-based plan for improving teaching, learning, and success in historically high-failure rate courses" (Gateways to Completion, 2017). In LCC's first 3-year cycle of this process (2013–2016), we focused on five courses: Principles of Accounting I; Foundations for Physiology; U.S. History, 1877 to Present; Intermediate Algebra; and Composition I. College faculty and staff enthusiastically engaged in the college-wide and course-level self-study using the embedded key performance indicators (KPIs), questions that help faculty and staff consider and apply evidence to answer teaching- and learning-related questions about the courses they teach. The answers to these questions formulated the basis for action plans that LCC faculty, working in a broad task force and individual course committees, then implemented.

One of LCC's college-level actions was to develop a method for faster delivery of student evaluations of instructors at the end of the semester. We were able to implement this change within 2 years by moving from paper to a completely online student–teacher evaluation system. A second college-level action focused on requiring all faculty to provide feedback "early and often" (Chickering & Gamson, 1987; Hattie & Timperley, 2007). This action was realized through the implementation of a new policy that requires faculty to use a centralized digital grading tool available to students on a 24/7 basis.

Course-level action plans for the first 3-year cycle of the process included the following:

- Principles of Accounting I:
  - Increasing access to tutoring and supplemental instruction
  - Providing more timely teacher feedback earlier in the semester
- Foundations for Physiology
  - Collaborating with Allied Health faculty to align learning outcomes across sections
  - Recruiting and retaining underrepresented student populations in biology
- U.S. History, 1877 to Present
  - Creating a course-wide syllabus review committee to ensure consistency across sections
  - Analyzing course assessment data to improve teaching and learning
- Intermediate Algebra
  - Designing and implementing a mentoring system for new instructors
  - Updating and disseminating the Math Library Guide
- Composition I
  - Revising learning outcomes
  - Identifying means of assessing learning outcomes

All of these recommendations were generated with extensive faculty involvement, which helps explain why they were adopted; because faculty generated the ideas, they were interested in seeing them implemented effectively.

We saw numerous positive results from our first G2C venture, including not only a new energy among faculty who were empowered to drive change, but also a drop in the online rates of Ds, Fs, withdrawals, and incompletes (DFWI rate) for these courses. We narrowed the achievement gap between students of color and White students in several classes as well, and during the project the DFWI rate overall dropped in biology, history, and writing. While there still is more work to do, our combining G2C with the Guided Pathways initiative has helped us greatly in sustaining the energy and desire among faculty to improve these courses.

Guided Pathways

Work in the 2017 Michigan Guided Pathways Institute pointed LCC toward the concepts of "meta-majors" (Waugh, 2016) and "maps." Maps are lists of classes in exact order that students must complete each semester in order to finish a program of study (major). A meta-major is a large category of careers relating to a central theme. For example, the communication meta-major includes careers like professional writer, journalist, social media designer, and web designer. Using meta-majors to help students design a broad degree plan and subsequently a specific map is antithetical to the traditional use of cafeteria-style models of course selection. Cafeteria models are pick-and-choose buffets of individual courses from which students create course schedules based on course availability, their schedules, and level of course difficulty (see Bailey, Jaggars & Jenkins, 2015a; Waugh, 2016) rather than on predetermined curricula linked to programs of study.

LCC established five meta-majors that were named by the students, "Career Communities." The State of Michigan's Career Clusters and Occupational Information Network (O*NET, 2017; see https://www.onetonline.org/) helped inform the creation of the Career Communities and allowed LCC to mesh data on occupations with its programs of study. The Career Communities are:

- Arts and Communications
- Business, Economics, and Management
- Computer, Engineering/Manufacturing, and Industrial Technology
- Health and Public Services
- Liberal Arts

Next, staff assigned each program of study to a Career Community and gave faculty time to respond to how their courses were placed and timed within their designated Career Community. The structure and alignment of the programs of study within these Career Communities were well received by LCC faculty at large; only a handful of revisions were suggested.

With the structure in place, faculty in programs of study began work on creating the program maps for their degrees. This task required getting the word out, specifically to faculty, as to what the phrase *guided pathways* actually meant and why LCC was involved in constructing them. Program maps were created for the ideal student—one who is full-time and requires no remediation. While full-time students are only a small fraction of our student body, this process helped LCC establish two things: the ideal sequencing of the courses for the program of study, and where general education courses best fit in support of the ideal program of study.

The most important part of the map creation tends to be the least discussed: ensuring that the courses in the map are worthwhile for students and supported by both the transfer-receiving institutions and eventual employers. This is hard work for many faculty members because it may require sacrificing a course they love to teach for a course needed for successful transfer or career opportunities. However, this concept was incorporated into the aforementioned conversations and workshops to achieve a consistent product for each program of study. Through using state online transfer resources, faculty became aware of the 4-year institutions that accepted their general education courses and those that did not.

While these activities were underway, LCC was advancing other important components of the Guided Pathways project. Predictable schedules—the product of using meta-majors and programs of study to organize a student's entire schedule at the start of the student's course work—were another component of the Guided Pathways work that LCC deemed important. Implementing predictable schedules at LCC meant that students working on an associate's degree would have a 2-year course schedule mapped out prior to the start of their first class. The guarantee that students could hold their seat in all their courses over a 2-year period was both a revolutionary and an evolutionary concept that resulted in the creation of a full pilot project in which we will be offering 1 year of scheduling for the 2018–2019 academic year, with appropriate testing and reconfiguring occurring during spring and summer 2018. This approach will allow the college to work out bugs before expanding to a full 2-year pilot.

Blending G2C and Guided Pathways

Starting in summer 2015, in response to the recognition of the possible benefits that could come from connecting gateway-course transformation and Guided Pathways efforts, LCC intentionally began blending its Guided Pathways and G2C efforts. This blending was accomplished in part because Rife and Conner, the authors of this chapter, each worked with one of the programs. We began meeting together regularly and collaborating on all aspects of the respective projects we were leading. Each of us became a member of the steering committee for the other's project, and we regularly shared drafts of documents, new ideas, and feedback with each other. It turned out, not surprisingly, that the faculty leaders who stepped forward to work on gateway courses were often the same faculty leaders who stepped forward to work on Guided Pathways. We were also able to identify a new cadre of early-adopting and innovative faculty to be involved in each of the projects. For the college, this was a significant benefit because it widened the pool of faculty leaders and brought new perspectives to each project. The benefits derived from the "cross-pollination" of the two projects cannot be understated. Many opportunities for faculty development and the generation of other student success initiatives have emanated from this blending.

Another way the two initiatives were blended occurred through increasing participant awareness of the potential connections through numerous workshops, presentations, and discussions. This active communication strategy helped address some of the ongoing concern faculty vocalized regarding "initiative overload," because efforts were made to show how the two projects were mutually reinforcing, as opposed to duplicative.

Guided Pathways and G2C advance two unique but compatible perspectives. First, it is just as important for G2C participants to understand the context of the program map as it is for the Guided Pathways participants to understand the impact of the "killer" (or gateway) course. Understanding exactly, for example, where Introduction to Sociology, a huge, multisection class at LCC, fits in various programs of study brings some dimension to the G2C course-transformation process that couldn't otherwise be realized. Second, understanding that high-risk gateway courses can undermine the best pathways, no matter how clear, effective, and efficient a program map might be, brings perspective to the Guided Pathways effort that would not have been realized had it not been for G2C. Having meetings and discussions with both groups together and systematic collaboration with the project leaders were crucial to assure that implemented institutional changes were complementary across projects. Working together intentionally created a more efficient and holistic approach to increasing student retention, completion, and transfer.

These efforts did not go unnoticed outside of the college. In summer 2015, 19 Michigan 2- and 4-year colleges and universities met and, as part of a broader statewide project planning meeting, learned how LCC accomplished connecting its Guided Pathways efforts with gateway-course redesign work. LCC's successes shared at this meeting helped the Gardner Institute partner with the Michigan Center for Student Success, and eight colleges and universities in the state received funding from the Kresge Foundation to launch the Michigan Gateways to Completion (Michigan G2C) project. Michigan G2C is bringing together three community colleges, including LCC, that were involved in the Michigan Guided Pathways Institute with the expressed goal of creating a more formalized method for connecting their Guided Pathways and gateway-course redesign work.

In this, LCC's second round of G2C, lessons from the Guided Pathways efforts are being used to identify three additional courses on which to focus. All of these courses are critical to specific pathways. The first, Pre-Calculus I, has been selected because it is a choice class for science, technology, engineering, and math (STEM) majors, many of whom wish to transfer to Michigan State University. LCC also selected Introduction to Sociology because of its high enrollment and high DFWI rate, in addition to a large achievement gap in this course between students of color and White students. Further, the class serves as a "global perspectives" requirement class for students obtaining an associate's degree from LCC. A third course had yet to be identified at the time of publication, but LCC will examine it similarly to ensure the broadest impact of redesign efforts.

By 2019, LCC will have spent 6 years working with laser-like focus on eight key gateway courses through G2C. Simultaneously, and complementarily, the college will also be in the sixth year of Guided

Pathways. Retrospectively, G2C was a great way to get LCC to focus on critical courses acting as barriers to students' success in various pathways. We have learned a great deal from our efforts—lessons that we believe have implications for others interested in doing similar work.

Lessons Learned and Recommendations for Future Work

A major change that came out of LCC's work to connect its course redesign and Guided Pathways efforts was the emphasis on and emergence of faculty leadership. We learned about the importance of strong encouragement from the provost for faculty and staff to become involved in campus-wide improvement efforts. LCC's provost continues to discuss the return on investment for providing faculty reassigned (or release) time to work on key projects at the college. In addition to making faculty feel valued and empowered, this emphasis also drew from the expertise and skill possessed by LCC faculty. Many faculty members were leaders in both projects, and as a result received reassigned time or, in the case of adjunct faculty, equivalent compensation.

The importance of one key lesson learned from these initiatives cannot be overemphasized: Institutions must plan for faculty support and reward. Additionally, it is better to overestimate the time such initiatives will take. Drawing as many faculty members as possible into leadership roles in projects of this nature, from across an array of disciplinary areas, and giving them time and rewards to undertake the work, create optimal conditions for success.

Another recommendation for future work involves intentionally overlapping and integrating student success initiatives in the manner described in this chapter. As many of us know from our own experiences, when various student success initiatives appear to be disconnected efforts, college employees will cry "Initiative overload!" However, through working to intentionally overlap the G2C and Guided Pathways efforts, LCC is experiencing success. The college has used its G2C work as a starting point for work with the Association of American Colleges and Universities (AAC&U). Through the grant-funded AAC&U Equity and Inclusive Excellence initiative, efforts are now focused specifically on two courses first examined in 2013 as high-DFWI gateway courses: U.S. History and Principles of Accounting I. The goal in the AAC&U initiative, pursuant to AAC&U guidelines, is to close the equity gap between African American/Black/Latino/a students and White students by 5% via the implementation of a summer institute conducted by LCC's chief diversity officer.

In the same trajectory, the hiring of 20 academic success coaches clearly is not an isolated student success initiative. It ties back to work connected to the Guided Pathways initiative, and the design asks that "students' progress based on academic plan is tracked, and frequent feedback is provided to them" (Jenkins, 2014, p. 5).

Another lesson learned that applies to future work at LCC and other colleges is that, regardless of the course or pathway, faculty and students have many of the same struggles and concerns. LCC's provost has held dozens of conversations with students and staff over the past several years. Time and time again, students have clearly articulated that they do not want to take even one course they do not need for their degree. This has led LCC to develop predictable 2-year scheduling, which again is a design suggested by Guided Pathways. Further, each class in the schedule should achieve excellence in learning and teaching, which is a G2C focus.

An additional lesson that will be applied to future work has to do with creating scalable methods and strategies for communication that help foster the desired change. Administrators know that, at a certain level, connections that are clear and understood in some corners of the institution are not clearly understood in other areas. There are still many at LCC who are unaware of the Guided Pathways and G2C projects, their connections, and what role they as individuals might play in these initiatives. To address this, LCC staff started working on creating the foundation for several project-integration summits that would be held for staff, faculty, and administrators to learn about the projects and how they work together to support each other toward students' ability to attain their completion or transfer goals. These summits will require the leads from several of the college's key student success projects—G2C, Guided Pathways, the recently started AAC&U Equity and Inclusive Excellence initiative, as well as an additional student portal project—to work together to inform the campus community with routine updates and breakout sessions. The summits will draw on a format that has been successful in the past: working lunches to foster connection with all stakeholder groups.

Finally, we recommend that everyone involved in efforts to integrate these (and other) student success initiatives appreciate the importance of patience and perspective. One likely outcome of overlapping initiatives is that the achievement of positive change will come a bit faster than if initiatives are siloed, or left to be administered without regard for other efforts on campus. We learned that when groups of faculty and others collaborate and band together, and ask for change via one or more cross-college groups, our asks are taken seriously and worked on/implemented. All of this, however, requires faculty and administrators to be willing to lead the way and do the necessary work. If these conditions are met, then most efforts are likely to succeed, just as they have at LCC.

References

Bailey, T., Jaggars, S. S., & Jenkins, D. (2015a). *Implementing Guided Pathways: Tips and tools*. New York, NY: Columbia University Teachers College, Community College Research Center.

Bailey, T., Jaggars, S., & Jenkins, D. (2015b). *Redesigning America's community colleges: A clearer path to student success.* Cambridge, MA: Harvard University Press.

Chickering, A. W., & Gamson, Z. F. (1987). Seven principles for good practice in undergraduate education. *AAHE Bulletin, 39*(1), 3–7.

Community College Research Center. (2015, March). *What we know about Guided Pathways.* Retrieved from http://ccrc.tc.columbia.edu/media/k2/attachments/What-We-Know-Guided-Pathways.pdf

Gateways to Completion. (2017). John N. Gardner Institute for Excellence in Undergraduate Education. Retrieved from http://www.jngi.org/g2c/

Hattie, J., & Timperley, H. (2007). The power of feedback. *Review of Educational Research, 77*(1), 81–112.

Hopkins, C. (2017, April). *Four-year colleges are using Guided Pathways, too—here's why.* Retrieved from https://www.eab.com/daily-briefing/2017/04/07/4-year-colleges-are-using-guided-pathways-too

Jenkins, D. (2014). *Redesigning community colleges for student success: Overview of the Guided Pathways approach.* New York, NY: Columbia University Teachers College, Community College Research Center. Retrieved from http://www.mcca.org/uploads/ckeditor/files/DavisJenkins_CCRC_Guided%20Pathways%20Overview_Revised%20Oct%202014.pdf

Michigan Community College Association (MCCA). (2017). *Guided Pathways resource repository.* Available from http://www.mcca.org/content.cfm?m=174&id=174&startRow=1&mm=0

O*NET Online. (2017). Retrieved from https://www.onetonline.org

Waugh, A. (2016). *Meta-majors: An essential first step on the path to college completion.* Boston, MA: Jobs for the Future. Retrieved from http://www.jff.org/publications/meta-majors-essential-first-step-path-college-completion

Martine Courant Rife is a professor of writing at Lansing Community College and is the Gateways to Completion liaison.

Christine Conner is the program faculty chair for fashion studies and Guided Pathways coordinator at Lansing Community College.

New Directions for Higher Education • DOI: 10.1002/he

9

Drawing on systems theory, this chapter uses two different institutional examples to demonstrate the benefits of combining gateway-course improvement initiatives with other student success efforts so that the combined approach makes the whole greater than the simple sum of the pieces.

Maximizing Gateway-Course Improvement by Making the Whole Greater Than the Sum of the Parts

Andrew K. Koch, Richard J. Prystowsky, Tony Scinta

The whole is more than the sum of its parts. So professed Aristotle nearly 2,400 years ago in *Metaphysics* (Sachs, 2002). In accordance with this Aristotelian view, the world and all of its beings must be considered as mutually interrelated parts of a purpose-yielding, organized whole. This whole has synergy that is born from interactions among myriad constituents. If these pieces are considered alone or never connected, the synergy is not yielded and the whole never revealed.

This classical notion is at the root of the concept of *holism* present in contemporary systems theory and its derivatives such as complexity and chaos theory commonly found in biology, psychology, and sociology (von Bertalanffy, 1972). Though it is beyond the scope of this chapter to trace the development of holism from the age of Aristotle to the present time, we should point out that holists from the classical era to today emphasize that complex systems—living or organizational—cannot be understood from a study of their properties or components in isolation. Something special happens between individual parts and/or persons working together in a cooperative, integrated whole.

It should come as no surprise that holist ideas that constitute the foundation of theory in contemporary biology, psychology, and sociology are also at play in what can be experienced in efforts to reform and reframe the gateway courses experienced in those or other disciplines. In short, when it comes to gateway-course transformation efforts, some of the most promising outcomes seem to occur when the efforts are intentionally combined to make the whole greater than its otherwise disparate components.

New Directions for Higher Education, no. 180, Winter 2017   © 2017 Wiley Periodicals, Inc.
Published online in Wiley Online Library (wileyonlinelibrary.com) • DOI: 10.1002/he.20265

This chapter provides two examples of systemic approaches to gateway-course transformation—efforts that focus on connecting pieces to intentionally yield outcomes and findings that would not have been possible if the components had been left to function on their own. One such effort, at Nevada State College, provides an example of the kinds of benefits that are feasible when an institution sets out to intentionally combine its active learning, peer support, and analytics efforts in a larger gateway-course improvement system. The second example, from Lansing Community College (LCC), shows what is possible when gateway-course redesign strategies are intentionally connected with other institutional-level student success efforts, such as a guided pathway initiative and an equity-minded practices project, to address broader institutional and societal completion goals. The examples show that this systems approach is applicable in both 2-year and 4-year postsecondary environments and serves as a model for emulation by other institutions also seeking to more meaningfully make the whole of their gateway-course improvement efforts greater than the sum of their parts.

Connecting the Parts at Nevada State College

Nevada State College (NSC) was founded in 2002 as a hopeful answer to the long-standing question of how to increase educational attainment in Nevada. Positioned between the state's universities and community colleges and guided by a steadfast commitment to exceptional teaching and learning, NSC strives to make a difference in the lives of students who, in many cases, never expected to attend college, much less earn a baccalaureate degree. NSC's mission is replete with opportunity, including the singular chance to build a modern institution from the ground up, but it also faces a host of challenges. The foremost obstacles, including deficits in funding, people, and college-ready students, are not unfamiliar to many colleges and universities. However, they are perhaps accentuated by the unusual circumstance of forging a college from scratch—of "building the ship while we sail it," as is often said by those who work at NSC. The net result is that, although the college has changed the lives of many students for the better, its overall retention and graduation rates fall short of its expectations.

Faced with these challenges, but inspired by the promise of its students, NSC partnered with the John N. Gardner Institute for Excellence in Undergraduate Education as one of the 13 founding institutions in the Gateways to Completion (G2C) project. NSC's collaboration was defined by two overarching goals: (1) to improve the student experience in gateway courses as an anticipated catalyst of long-term college success and (2) to narrow equity gaps involving student populations that have been historically underrepresented in college. Two underlying principles facilitated the pursuit of these goals, and both run to the core of the college's institutional DNA. First, data and evidence would be the effort's guiding light, informing decisions, shaping curricula, and driving improvement. Second, the college aimed to successfully integrate the work of academic faculty and student affairs professionals. This latter approach partly reflected the structure of NSC's campus, which eschews traditional silos in favor of intentional collaboration, but also responded to the college's experience with erstwhile initiatives, which showed that great teaching is not enough, on its own, to achieve desired increases in student success.

Since launching the G2C program in fall 2014, NSC's faculty and staff have observed significant overall increases in retention and academic performance among participating students. Importantly, the magnitude of this effect generally has been larger among first-generation and under represented students (Patterson, 2017). The paragraphs that follow describe how the college founded, developed, and implemented the program and highlight the challenges and future directions that emerged along the way.

Like many of NSC's more successful initiatives, the G2C program was built on a robust foundation of qualitative and quantitative data. Using a best-practices framework furnished by the Gardner Institute, the college conducted an intensive—and often daunting—self-assessment of institutional characteristics, from the presence of early warning systems and learning communities to the nature of tutoring and advising services.

The assessment revealed several kinks in NSC's institutional armor, but two consistent patterns stood in stark relief against a constellation of data points. First, as NSC's faculty and staff might have predicted, learning experiences matter, and the ones that promote student success tend to be grounded in meaningful questions and real-world contexts. Second, use of academic support services was strongly and positively correlated with favorable student outcomes. Students who used advising, frequented office hours, and leveraged tutoring support exhibited better grades and retention rates than those who did not. The correlational analysis raised the specter of a third variable—perhaps only better-prepared students sought out these support networks—but deeper analysis revealed that the impact of these services was even stronger among students who had struggled in high school. Unfortunately, a companion analysis cast a shadow over this finding: Among NSC students, the utilization of these services was astoundingly low (Patterson, 2017). For example, the percentage of students who used the tutoring center varied from one semester to the next, but never climbed into double digits.

This narrative was disappointing but oddly encouraging to NSC's faculty and staff: They felt if they could simply increase student engagement with these support systems, good things would happen. With this prospect in mind, the college set out to simultaneously enhance the learning experience and increase student access to student support. What the participating faculty and staff did not realize at the time was that both would happen in the same place: the classroom.

Initially, the college needed to determine how it could create something of this scale. The ship being built does not sail itself, and the participating NSC stakeholders reluctantly acknowledged that the fall and spring semesters would not be ideal times to ask overtaxed faculty members to don their innovation caps and create an ambitious program. Consequently, the college made a big decision and a bigger investment: It created a summer institute where faculty on 9-month contracts would receive a stipend to develop the initiative during the summer term, with a planned implementation the following fall. The summer institute covered 8 weeks, with two 3-hour workshops each week. The G2C liaison—the leader of the G2C project at NSC—and a mentor from the Gardner Institute helped guide participating faculty and staff through the initiative, providing framing evidence, feedback on program development, and efforts to resolve difficult questions as they unfolded.

Importantly, unlike many prior efforts, NSC did not rely exclusively on its outstanding faculty to develop the program; rather, the college brought together professors from multiple disciplines (for example, math, psychology, and biology) with key academic support personnel from advising, tutoring, and NSC's writing center. The work of the entire team was unified by the utilization of evidence, including emerging findings about noncognitive factors such as social belonging (Stephens, Hamedani, & Destin, 2014) and sound internal data on student success, such as the aforementioned findings regarding student support services.

Consistent with the college's initial goals, two major program elements defined the initiative. The first was the curriculum redesign of five gateway courses with an emphasis on empowering students to address real-world issues. For example, with the redesigned college math course for nonscience majors, the math faculty excised elements that were less likely to benefit the general student population, such as algebraic knowledge that mainly serves as a stepping-stone to a calculus class they will never take, and replaced it with content that is more likely to surface in daily life, including statistics, financial knowledge, and probability. For NSC's college composition course, the faculty scoured best practices and cultivated a new approach to "writing about writing" that emphasized metacognition and the empowering influence a writer can wield with important real-world audiences. In the college success/first-year seminar course, the final project challenged students to devise a way to improve Nevada State College for later review by the office of the provost.

As the curriculum development progressed, faculty and staff contemplated how they could engage more students in their academic support services. Early in the process, the participating faculty and staff succumbed to an emotion that is uncommon at NSC: pessimism. Saddled with the logistics of a 100% commuter population and the single-digit participation rates for many support centers, the college's G2C team recognized the folly of trying to encourage droves of students to suddenly use academic support. Consequently, they invented a means of bringing the support directly to the students. Importantly, the faculty and staff did not merely want to integrate tutoring support into the student experience; they wanted this support to be wrapped in the noncognitive literature that offers an increasingly effective prescription for the success of students who are historically underrepresented in higher education (Yeager & Walton, 2011). The resulting innovation was the course assistant (CA), a successful, experienced student who played the hybrid role of embedded tutor, supplemental instruction (SI) leader, and peer mentor. (For more on the CA program, see Chapter 4 in this volume.) The embedded component meant that the CAs sat in on every session of the gateway course to which they were assigned, cataloging where students struggled and often participating in class activities. The SI sessions allowed the CAs to develop and implement lesson plans that addressed challenging topics, and the peer mentor component equipped CAs with a working knowledge of factors such as social belonging and academic mind-set, and asked them to help students overcome the many nonacademic obstacles encountered in college.

The development of this new role also yielded one of the biggest unexpected dividends of the entire G2C initiative. To properly cultivate CAs, the college engineered a 4-day training sequence that married evidence-based principles with intensive, hands-on training. Though the training initially focused on NSC's first cohort of 11 CAs, it has since been expanded to peer support specialists from every corner of campus and now reaches more than 60 student workers in the most recent iteration.

Though NSC's faculty and staff are roundly pleased with the results of the G2C initiative, they certainly encountered their share of headaches—and heartache—along the way. One of the foremost lessons taught the college that a collaborative effort may be ideal for building an initiative like the CA program, but it is not an advisable way to lead the effort. Consequently, NSC has created a CA coordinator position to provide oversight of the program and help iron out the day-to-day wrinkles that have threatened to derail the initiative. Likewise, NSC achieved favorable initial results with the redesigned gateway courses, but in some cases it was difficult to maintain this success, largely because the people who orchestrated the initiative were called to address other campus issues after the inaugural semester. NSC has yet to uncover a magic elixir for this challenge, but communication and coordination among key stakeholders have aided the cause.

Given the effectiveness of the initiative, the foremost goal for the future development of the efforts at NSC is to continue to grow the CA program and extend its impact to an ever-larger population of students. However, the college would also be well served to include more student workers—and even faculty and staff—in the peer support training that has worked so well to date, thereby giving a progressively larger contingent of NSC constituents a sound, evidence-based foundation for supporting and guiding students. The college is also shifting the lens of assessment from the students who receive student support to the CAs who provide it. The goal is twofold: to better understand the positive development experienced by CAs and to diagnose and treat the challenges they face in striving to balance their own academic pursuits against the needs of the students under their care.

Moving Past the Sum of the Parts at LCC

For the past several years, LCC has been engaged in a comprehensive, institutionally transformative student success initiative entitled Operation 100%. The goal of this initiative is 100% completion for students in certificate, degree, or transfer pathways. Serving as both a metric of achievement and an attitude underlying the college's approach to continuous student success-oriented improvement, Operation 100% is driven by the intention that all students will leave LCC with their educational dreams fulfilled.

Operation 100% entails a variety of projects related to academic work and wraparound student support services. For example, LCC has hired a cadre of academic success coaches, whose singular, laser-focused mission is to help students successfully complete courses and programs. The college also introduced a class scheduling tool that provides various options tailored to meet students' particular scheduling needs. This tool will integrate into an automated registration process designed to ensure that students remain on track toward certificate, degree, or transfer completion. To complement this work, the college is developing a 2-year master schedule that will allow students to lock in all of their courses for the entirety of their certificate or degree programs. More broadly, the next iteration of the college's strategic plan is being developed with Operation 100% as its guiding star, and its revised mission statement derives in large part from Operation 100%'s ongoing and projected work. In short, wide-ranging in reach and intentionally cross-functional in practice, Operation 100% purposefully interweaves projects into a strong fabric of student success design (Prystowsky, Koch, & Baldwin, 2015).

Catalytic to the successful launch of Operation 100% was LCC's participation as a founding college in the Gardner Institute's G2C gateway-course transformation initiative. Already experienced in helping to launch a cutting-edge, collaborative student success initiative, a number of LCC's G2C faculty joined teams of others from various areas of the college to help develop major components of Operation 100% early in the work; to this day, a number of these faculty members remain leaders in Operation 100%. As LCC engaged in the initial stages of this work, its faculty and staff saw the benefits of continuing, from the beginning, to develop otherwise disparate student success projects in an integrative manner. This mind-set helped the faculty and staff see that their chances of helping all students in degree, certificate, or transfer pathways achieve their completion goals would be greatly enhanced if their G2C work was incorporated into the work of creating well-designed program pathways, which would allow students to explore options but would not, however inadvertently, impede students' progress toward goal completion. The college further bolstered this effort when it joined other community colleges in Michigan as members of the first cohort of 2-year schools participating in Michigan's Guided Pathways Institute and, not long afterward, when it joined community colleges around the nation as participants in the American Association of Community Colleges' national Pathways Project.

The interweaving of LCC's G2C and Guided Pathways projects remains foundational to the ongoing strengthening of Operation 100%. Buttressing the larger and smaller components of this initiative, this intertwined work has confirmed for LCC's faculty and staff the value of intentionally integrating student success efforts. Doing otherwise might unwittingly undermine the college's efforts to help students. This possibility became readily apparent to LCC's faculty and staff when, in the early stages of their efforts, they asked themselves these two questions:

1. How valuable would successful completion of gateway courses ultimately be to a student who, lost amid confusing paths and choices, remains far from his or her goal of completing a degree or certificate or of transferring to a 4-year school?

2. How likely would a student be to achieve a degree or certificate, or to transfer to a 4-year school, were she or he unable to pass gateway courses that are either within or prerequisite to her or his program pathway?

Integrating these otherwise ostensibly separate projects thus seemed a sine qua non in the college's quest to achieve success with Operation 100%.

Perhaps not surprisingly, faculty and staff involved in the effort at LCC also discovered that integrating and complementing the otherwise seemingly isolated work of G2C and Guided Pathways has led to further strengthening the development of other collaborative student success efforts. For example, faculty have begun investigating ways to deliver programs' general education courses in a nondistributive, integrated fashion so that students would be able to achieve course- and program-level competencies in applied, increasingly meaningful ways. This exploration will eventuate in, among other outcomes, integrated learning opportunities for students coenrolled in sections of courses (for instance, linked sections of a writing and a science course), increased team teaching scenarios, and the creation of integrated interdisciplinary or cross-disciplinary block scheduling. Like the G2C and Guided Pathways initiatives, the effort to infuse integrated learning throughout program pathways is led by faculty. Not surprisingly, faculty professional development has benefited greatly from all of these efforts, and cross-disciplinary collaboration has begun to strengthen considerably.

NEW DIRECTIONS FOR HIGHER EDUCATION • DOI: 10.1002/he

Ultimately, all of this work is intended to bolster student success. In this regard, the drop in rates of Ds, Fs, withdrawals, and incompletes (DFWI) resulting from LCC's G2C work bodes well for both increased retention rates and increased completion. However, as the college continues to examine its data, faculty and staff remain concerned that equity gaps for students from underserved groups will not be sufficiently closed. Ameliorating this problem will help LCC ensure that all of its students attain their completion goals. In addition, and perhaps even more importantly, it will also help the college's faculty and staff keep their sometimes tacit but nonetheless real commitment to serve the needs of students who, facing obstacles to their achieving success in school, need champions and have come to the college's faculty and staff for help. The faculty and staff firmly believe that it is simply a matter of conscience that the college does everything that it can to help these students.

To this end, LCC is engaged in an equity-minded initiative launched by the Association of American Colleges and Universities entitled Committing to Equity and Inclusive Excellence. This 2-year, grant-funded initiative strives to help colleges and universities close equity gaps while delivering high-quality education to all students. For their part, LCC has set a goal of closing equity gaps for African American males and females and for Latinas and Latinos by 5% by the end of the second year of the grant. Seeing this effort as a proof-of-concept undertaking, LCC plans to use lessons learned to strengthen its equity-related work more broadly at the college.

The college's work on gateway courses has proved invaluable to the foundational and initial success of its equity project (which is also faculty-led). Already engaged in efforts to lower DFWI rates for students from underserved populations, the G2C process helped the college faculty conceptualize the larger framework for closing equity gaps at LCC. Two of these faculty members also helped the college make a crucial discovery: In their college-level gateway classes, the problem related to lowering the DFWI rates for students from underserved groups is not so much that these rates remain too high (the samples are relatively small); rather, too few students from these groups are enrolled in the gateway courses at the start of the term.

As LCC has begun to address this problem, its faculty and staff are hopeful that their efforts will help to ameliorate other equity-related issues or problems at the college as well. To these ends, the college has taken various actions, including accelerating the time (without sacrificing quality) in which students move from developmental education classes to college-level classes (students from underserved groups tend to be disparately affected by placement into developmental education classes). The college has also begun conceptualizing a pipeline for kindergarten through 12th-grade students to enroll in its college-level gateway biology class (this is one of the classes with low enrollment of students from underserved groups). More broadly, knowing that LCC needs to address the implicit biases that faculty and staff bring to their work if it is to succeed in closing equity gaps (no one is immune from having implicit biases), and understanding that everyone at the college plays a role in helping students succeed, the institution has begun implicit bias-awareness training for both faculty and staff. Finally, recognizing the central role played by faculty in student success, the college has created Faculty Institutes for those teaching gateway courses. Led by the college's chief diversity officer, these Institutes are aimed at helping faculty maximize their engagement with all students, to be sure, but especially with students most at risk of not succeeding in the course. Preliminary qualitative results make the LCC community hopeful that, in the aggregate, these and other equity-minded actions will lead to greater retention and completion rates for students from underserved populations and ultimately will serve as model practices enabling faculty to help *all* LCC students achieve their completion goals (Prystowsky & Heutsche, in press).

The work undertaken for the equity project has yielded a once tacit, but now explicit, vision statement for Operation 100%: "100% Success Through 100% Inclusion." Underscoring all of the college's student success efforts, this vision encapsulates LCC's belief that, as intimated earlier, as a matter of conscience the college's faculty and staff are obligated to do whatever they can to help all of the college's students in certificate, degree, or transfer pathways achieve their completion goals. LCC's students have entrusted their educational dreams to the college and its educators. The college's faculty and staff, in turn, believe that they owe them the best of LCC's efforts—and they are striving to do their best through Operation 100% and its many intentionally connected components, including its G2C gateway-course transformation efforts.

Summary and Conclusions

Systems are, by definition, parts in interaction. They consist of "organized complexities" that bring about strong, nontrivial synergies. The synergies derived from a system can, in turn, yield greater outcomes than what would have naturally occurred if their parts had remained isolated and disconnected (von Bertalanffy, 1972). In short, there is a strong relationship between structure and behavior, and systems are designed to purposefully yield desired behavior and outcomes (Meadows, 2008).

These strong relationships are evident in the gateway-course transformation efforts—or systems—described in this chapter. At Nevada State College, faculty and staff worked together to foster greater interaction and connection between various academic support, instructional design, and course redesign efforts. In the process, they created a subsystem—a subcomponent of their broader organization of which it is a part—in which the relationships between the subsystem's parts have become stronger in pursuit of a shared purpose. At LCC, the gateway course redesign subsystem has been linked with its Guided Pathways subsystem, its equity and inclusive excellence subsystem, and other components to yield a new student success ecosystem—a higher-level (in a hierarchical sense) system that LCC has named Operation 100%.

Regardless of their hierarchical structure, these systems exist to address issues of suboptimization—the condition in which the function of a part of a system limits the goals or function of the system as a whole (Meadows, 2008). Nevada State College is using its G2C gateway-course transformation efforts to optimize student learning and success in five of its high-risk courses. LCC is doing the same, but it is also using its G2C efforts to optimize the outcomes associated with other subsystems and the broader student success ecosystem of which these subsystems all are a part.

It is important to point out that optimization as it is used in systems theory is not simply about finances. In fact, it may have little to do with money at all. As the systems theorist Stanford Beer (2002) noted, the purpose of a system is what it does. At LCC and Nevada State College, the gateway-course transformation systems and the ecosystems of which they are a part exist for the purpose of mitigating inequitable outcomes in courses and in the pathways of which these courses are a part. As described in both the LCC and NSC stories presented in this chapter, both of these colleges have created new systems to address forms of systemic inequity that existed in their previous structures.

This is why what LCC and NSC are doing with their gateway-course efforts truly matters. Simply stated, by intentionally ensuring that the whole be meaningfully (and, where appropriate, measurably) greater than the sum of the parts, these colleges are taking additional steps to further mitigate inequitable outcomes for historically underserved and underrepresented students. In doing so, these institutions are better able to serve their learners and the communities of which these learners are a part.

References

Beer, S. (2002). What is cybernetics? *Kybernetes, 31*(2), 209–219.

Meadows, D. H. (2008). *Thinking in systems: A primer.* White River Junction, VT: Chelsea Green Publishing.

Patterson, B. (2017, March). *Performance metrics, Nevada State College.* Presentation conducted at the quarterly meeting of the Nevada Board of Regents.

Prystowsky R., & Heutsche, A. M. (in press). Facing ourselves, engaging our students: Equity-minded practices at work, *AAC&U Peer Review.*

Prystowsky, R., Koch, A. K., & Baldwin, C. (2015, Fall). Operation 100%, or, completion by redesign. *AAC&U Peer Review,* 19–22.

Sachs, J. (Trans.) (2002). *Aristotle's Metaphysics* (2nd ed.). Santa Fe, NM: Green Lion Press.

Stephens, N. M., Hamedani, M. G., & Destin, M. (2014). Closing the social-class achievement gap: A difference-education intervention improves first-generation students' academic performance and all students' college transition. *Psychological Science, 25*(4), 943–953.

von Bertalanffy, L. (1972). The history and status of general systems theory. *Academy of Management Journal, 15*(4), 407–426.

Yeager, D. S., & Walton, G. M. (2011). Social-psychological interventions in education: They're not magic. *Review of Educational Research, 81*(2), 267–301.

Andrew K. Koch is the president and chief operating officer of the nonprofit John N. Gardner Institute for Excellence in Undergraduate Education, located in Brevard, North Carolina.

Richard J. Prystowsky is the former provost and senior vice president for academic and student affairs at Lansing Community College in Michigan.

Tony Scinta is the vice provost for academic innovation and student success and an associate professor of psychology at Nevada State College.

Index

Abdallah, C. T., 26, 27
Academic discipline associations and gateway-course, 75–77; beginning college history, 82–83; history, 81–82; history teaching, 77–79; mobilizing faculty members, 83–84; tuning project, 79–80
Access to Success (A2S), 45
Adelman, C., 14
Aitken, N., 36
Ambrose, S. A., 69
American Association of Community Colleges (AACC), 90
American Historical Association (AHA), 12, 75
Analytics, defined, 21
Arendale, D., 68, 69
Arendale, D. R., 43, 44, 47, 49
Arnold, K., 22, 24, 25, 26
Arnold, K. E., 21, 22, 23
Artze-Vega, I., 53, 62
Association for Institutional Research (AIR), 32
Association of American Colleges and Universities (AAC&U), 95
Astin, A. W., 25

Babbitt, T., 27
Bailey, T., 54, 90, 92
Bailey, T. R., 7
Bain, K., 71
Baker, R. S., 24
Bakharia, A., 23
Baldwin, C., 104
Barefoot, B. O., 12
Beer, S., 108
Berg, E. A., 31, 40
Birnbaum, R., 31
Bischel, J., 21
Blackboard Collaborate, 46
Bliss, L., 45
Bonham, B., 45
Boyer, E. L., 7
Boylan, H. R., 45
Bransberger, P., 15
Braxton, J. M., 15, 64
Bridges, M. W., 69
Brookins, J., 75, 78, 81, 85

Brooklyn College, 69
Brown, M. G., 21, 22
Brown University, 44

Calder, L., 78, 82
Campbell, J. P., 21, 22
Carey, E., 79
Carleton College, 44, 54
Carleton's model, 44
Caulkins, J., 53, 62
Caulkins, J. L., 55
Center for Excellence in Teaching and Learning (CETL), 48
Center for the Advancement of Teaching (CAT), 56
Centers for teaching and learning (CTL), 70
Check My Activity, 26
Chickering, A.W., 25, 91
Chief academic officers (CAO) and gateway courses, 63–64, 69–70; allies and leaders, 64; CAO roundup, 70–71; deconstructing silos, 67–68; disciplinary organizations, 70; identifying and reviewing, 66–67; outreach to students, 68–69; sharing data, 64–66
Ciccone, A., 70
City University of New York, 69
Civil Rights Act, 12
Clow, D., 22
College Reading and Learning Association's (CRLA), 46
Columbia University, 89
Condon, W., 48, 54
Conner, C., 89, 97
Cooper, T. A., 79
Corbett, A. T., 24
Corrigan, K., 59
Corrin, L., 23
Corroy, J., 48
Couret, J., 55
Course assistant (CA), 47, 103
Cowley, K., 47
Cruce, T. M., 36
Cutright, M., 12

Daffinrud, S., 37, 38
Dawson, P., 47

111

University of Nevada Reno, 46
University of New Mexico, 27
University of Rhode Island (URI), 54–56
University of Wisconsin–Madison, 49
University of Wisconsin–Milwaukee (UWM), 45–46
Upcraft, M. L., 12
U.S. Department of Education, 14, 56
U.S. higher education, 43

van Barneveld, A., 21
Van der Meer, J., 47
Van de Ven, A., 31
Visual Basic for Application (VBA), 34
Voelker, D. J., 81, 82
Volkwein, J. F., 32
von Bertalanffy, L., 99, 107
Voorhees, R. A., 32

Walton, G. M., 103
Washington State University, 54
Waugh, A., 92
Wells, R., 15
Wenderoth, M. P., 15
Wiese, D., 37, 38
Wiggins, G., 70
Willett, G., 54
Willis, J. E., III, 22
Wilson, K., 25, 26
Wineburg, S., 78, 82
Wise, A. F., 25, 26
Wood, A., 58
Wu, D., 60

Yeager, D. S., 103

Zawacki, T., 47

SAY HELLO TO YOUR INCOMING CLASS
THEY'RE NOT MILLENNIALS ANYMORE

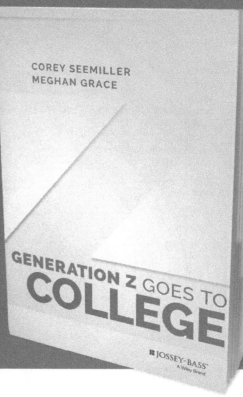

COREY SEEMILLER
MEGHAN GRACE

GENERATION Z GOES TO COLLEGE

JOSSEY-BASS
A Wiley Brand

Generation Z is rapidly replacing Millennials on college campuses. Those born 1995–2010 have different motivations, learning styles, characteristics, skill sets, and social concerns than previous generations. Unlike Millennials, these students grew up in a recession and are under few illusions. *Generation Z Goes to College* is the first book on how this up-and-coming generation will change higher education, reporting findings from an in-depth study of over 1,100 college students from 15 vastly different higher education institutions.

FIND OUT WHAT YOUR NEXT INCOMING CLASS IS ALL ABOUT.

JB JOSSEY-BASS™
A Wiley Brand

NEW DIRECTIONS FOR HIGHER EDUCATION

ORDER FORM SUBSCRIPTION AND SINGLE ISSUES

DISCOUNTED BACK ISSUES:

Use this form to receive 20% off all back issues of *New Directions for Higher Education*.
All single issues priced at **$23.20** (normally $29.00)

TITLE	ISSUE NO.	ISBN
_____	_____	_____
_____	_____	_____
_____	_____	_____

*Call 1-800-835-6770 or see mailing instructions below. When calling, mention the promotional code JBNND to receive
your discount. For a complete list of issues, please visit www.wiley.com/WileyCDA/WileyTitle/productCd-HE.html*

SUBSCRIPTIONS: (1 YEAR, 4 ISSUES)

☐ New Order   ☐ Renewal

U.S.	☐ Individual: $89	☐ Institutional: $356
Canada/Mexico	☐ Individual: $89	☐ Institutional: $398
All Others	☐ Individual: $113	☐ Institutional: $434

*Call 1-800-835-6770 or see mailing and pricing instructions below.
Online subscriptions are available at www.onlinelibrary.wiley.com*

ORDER TOTALS:

Issue / Subscription Amount: $ _____

Shipping Amount: $ _____
(for single issues only – subscription prices include shipping)

Total Amount: $ _____

SHIPPING CHARGES:

First Item	$6.00
Each Add'l Item	$2.00

*(No sales tax for U.S. subscriptions. Canadian residents, add GST for subscription orders. Individual rate subscriptions must
be paid by personal check or credit card. Individual rate subscriptions may not be resold as library copies.)*

BILLING & SHIPPING INFORMATION:

☐ **PAYMENT ENCLOSED:** *(U.S. check or money order only. All payments must be in U.S. dollars.)*

☐ **CREDIT CARD:**   ☐ VISA   ☐ MC   ☐ AMEX

Card number _____Exp. Date_____

Card Holder Name_____Card Issue #_____

Signature _____Day Phone_____

☐ **BILL ME:** *(U.S. institutional orders only. Purchase order required.)*

Purchase order # _____
Federal Tax ID 13559302 • GST 89102-8052

Name_____

Address_____

Phone_____ E-mail_____

Copy or detach page and send to: **John Wiley & Sons, Inc. / Jossey Bass
PO Box 55381
Boston, MA 02205-9850**

PROMO JBNND